BETRAYAL
of TRUST

BETRAYAL
of TRUST

*Confronting
and Preventing
Clergy Sexual
Misconduct*

Second Edition

STANLEY J. GRENZ
AND ROY D. BELL

BakerBooks

A Division of Baker Book House Co
Grand Rapids, Michigan 49516

© 1995 by Stanley J. Grenz and Roy D. Bell

Published by Baker Books
a division of Baker Book House Company
P.O. Box 6287, Grand Rapids, MI 49516-6287

New edition published 2001

Previously published by InterVarsity Press

Printed in the United States of America

Library of Congress Cataloging-in-Publication Data

Grenz, Stanley, 1950–
    Betrayal of trust : confronting and preventing clergy sexual misconduct / Stanley J. Grenz and Roy D. Bell.—2nd ed.
       p.   cm.
    Includes bibliographical references.
    ISBN 0-8010-9114-4 (pbk.)
    1. Clergy—United States—Sexual behavior. 2. Sex crimes—United States. 3. Clergy—Professional ethics. I. Bell, Roy D. II. Title.
BV4392.G74   2001
253'.2—dc21   2001035206

For current information about all releases from Baker Book House, visit our web site:
http://www.bakerbooks.com

Contents

To
Phil Collins
dedicated pastor,
effective administrator,
dependable friend

Preface

Every pastor is the recipient of a sacred trust. A minister often becomes a symbol of the Christian faith in the eyes of many people, both in the congregation and in the wider community. As a consequence, people generally expect pastors to be models of integrity. More important, congregants entrust themselves to the minister's spiritual care.

Effective ministry can occur only within a climate of trust—only when congregants believe that their pastor will always seek their spiritual benefit. And the connection between trust and ministry means that a betrayal of this trust destroys the very conditions that make genuine ministry possible.

Perhaps no betrayal of trust has worked more devastation than clergy sexual misconduct. The time has come for the church to address this grave problem, which threatens the very foundations for Christian ministry.

We believe that sexual misconduct in the pastorate is such a debilitating problem because it marks a twofold betrayal of trust. It betrays a sacred sexual trust, and it constitutes an abuse of power. Recent literature regularly explores the second dimension. But thinkers have been reticent to address the first.

Through our own ministry in the church, we have become all too familiar with the phenomenon of sexual failure among ministers. We have seen its devastating impact. And we are acutely aware of the tragedies that unfold when a betrayal of trust takes place. Like ripples from a stone dropped in a pond, the devastation engulfs a widening circle of people—the pastor and the congregant, their spouses and children, the congregation and eventually the larger church, as well as the wider community.

As the title *Betrayal of Trust* suggests, we seek to present sexual misconduct in the pastorate as the betrayal of a sexual and a power trust. Our goal, however, is not to point a self-righteous finger, affix undue blame or add insult to injury. We are all susceptible to failure, and we are all affected when one member of the "family" suffers. Therefore, we desire to serve as catalysts for reflection, for heartfelt repentance, for correction and positive change, and for prevention.

Clergy sexual misconduct encompasses many behaviors. Rather than deal with its various expressions, we have carefully chosen to limit the scope of our discussion to what we believe is the most widespread problem among evangelical churches: sexual involvement between a male pastor and a female congregant. Although not the whole story, it is this scenario that at this point in history has emerged as the most devastating to the churches we serve.

The focus on male pastor and female congregant explains what may appear to be our archaic use of the pronoun *he* to refer to the minister. This word choice should not be interpreted as suggesting that only males can be pastors. Nor does it indicate a blindness to the reality of *female* clergy sexual misconduct. We speak of the pastor as "he" and the congregant as "she" simply because we want to focus the lens of our discussion on this specific dimension of what is admittedly a broader phenomenon.

We should also explain that we have been careful throughout not to divulge any confidences or carelessly pass along accounts of actual incidents of abuse by clergy. So we have frequently altered certain details, created composite stories drawing on several different accounts, and so forth.

Betrayal of Trust was born out of our discovery in spring 1994 that we share a concern for the evangelical church, which is increasingly losing its credibility in society. We are convinced that the debilitating problem of sexual misconduct among pastors is a major factor in this erosion of credibility.

Our collegial relationship at Carey Theology College in Vancouver, British Columbia, provided the context in which we were made cognizant of this and other shared concerns. We deeply appreciate the opportunities that being on the Carey faculty has given us to think together, work together and pray together. And we acknowledge the important support the college has offered to this project. Tangible support included the secretarial assistance of Beverley Norgren and the "nuts and bolts" help we received from our research assistant, Rob Ogilvie.

For over a decade, Carey Theological College was ably guided by Phil Collins, its principal. In August 1994 Dr. Collins relinquished the helm of the school. In honor of his retirement and in appreciation for his ministry and friendship—of which we, together with many others, have been the recipients—we dedicate this book to him.

Preface to the Second Edition

Betrayal of Trust first appeared in 1995. Events during the intervening years have indicated that the issues we raised then have not disappeared. On the contrary, the concerns that initially motivated us to write this volume are even more crucial today than they were during the waning years of the twentieth century.

Perhaps no event did more to catapult into the public conscience the glaring reality of sexual misconduct among leaders than the escapades of then-President Bill Clinton. His philandering nearly cost him the presidency. The philandering spirit is especially debilitating, however, when it occurs among church leaders. It is not surprising, therefore, that the revelation of sexual misconduct involving the president of a leading seminary in the United States cost the perpetrator his position at the helm of this institution dedicated to the training of future pastors. The betrayal of such a sacred trust is not an exclusively North American problem. The case of the British evangelical leader who left his wife to pursue a relationship with a young man in his congregation sent shock waves not only through the United Kingdom but around the world as well. Events such as these are just the tip of the iceberg, especially when local churches and parachurch ministries come into view. We are in the midst of a crisis that threatens the public reputation of the church as a whole. Regardless of the nationality, location on the theological landscape or denominational affiliation of the persons involved, the gospel of Jesus Christ is tarnished whenever those who supposedly have committed their lives to the proclamation of the Good News reveal that they have built their spiritual house on the sand.

It is our hope that the second edition of *Betrayal of Trust* will spark a renewed awareness of the gravity of the problem of clergy sexual misconduct. In addition, however, we are convinced that the implementation of a proactive process, such as is outlined in these pages, could serve to combat the disturbing incidence of pastors overstepping the boundaries of wholesome relationships with persons in their care. How can the church rest when a congregant is more likely to fall victim to a pastor entrusted with the sacred task of caring for Christ's flock than to a secular therapist?

To this end, we have added an eighth chapter that focuses specifically on the "wanderer." We are convinced that preventive measures initiated by and for the sake of those who are prone to cross into the "forbidden zone" or who have violated their sacred trust in an unpremeditated manner can function as a necessary first step in gaining complete victory over the larger debilitating problem. And the victory toward which we have dedicated our efforts in this volume is not only for the sake of the church of Jesus Christ but also on behalf of those who so desperately need to see the gospel embodied in the lives of those who claim to be Christ's disciples.

Readying the second edition has reminded us of the book's obvious shortcoming, namely, its brevity. As we indicated in the preface to the first edition, a book of this type cannot address every dimension of clergy sexual misconduct. To deal adequately with the full breadth of the problem would require a volume several times the size of *Betrayal of Trust*. Rather, we have chosen to tackle here the situation that continues to account for the vast majority of cases and that we therefore believe remains the most crucial concern of the church today. Doing so, however, means that we not only pass over other variations of the difficulty but also by necessity make the assumption both in the pronouns we use and the perspective from which we present the content that clergy are male. This narrowing of focus ought not to be read as a prescription for, or even a description of, the ministerial office in the church. (Indeed, our views on the theological issue of women in ministry are well known.) On the contrary, *Betrayal of Trust* is written from the perspective of male clergy (and, to a lesser extent, married clergy) in order to address more easily the specific problem of male pastors (who are generally married) becoming sexually involved with female congregants.

Finally, we express our gratitude to Robert Hosack of Baker Book House, who was instrumental in bringing to fruition our desire to offer a second edition of this book.

Introduction

In 1868 Henry Ward Beecher (1813-1887), the renowned pastor of Plymouth Congregational Church in Brooklyn Heights, New York, began visiting Elizabeth Tilton, a congregant and the wife of a close friend. He hoped to console her on the death of her child. Their relationship continued, however, until several years later rumors of impropriety led Elizabeth Tilton's husband to lay charges against the pastor. Despite overwhelming evidence of their pastor's guilt, Plymouth Church stood by him. In 1878 the congregation excommunicated those who had testified against Beecher, including Elizabeth Tilton. She died in 1897, ostracized and alone.

As the Beecher case indicates, sexual abuse is not just a recent phenomenon. Nevertheless, since the 1980s it has emerged as a major problem in North American society.

Although clergy sexual misconduct has grabbed the headlines, the problem of professionals sexually abusing clients is not unique to the Christian church. It has reached epidemic proportions in most of the caregiving professions.

A recent survey conducted by *Psychology Today* revealed that 7 to 12 percent of psychologists, psychiatrists, social workers and other therapists admitted to being involved in sexual misconduct.[1] A 1992 survey of medical practitioners yielded the same results: 9 percent of family doctors, internists, gynecologists and surgeons had engaged in sexual misconduct with patients.[2] The College of Physicians and Surgeons in Ontario, Canada, established a task force to research the extent of sexual abuse by their members. Within six weeks of its launching, the head of the enquiry, Marilou McPhedran, reported being "shocked by the magnitude of the problem."[3] Hundreds of Ontario residents had flooded them with complaints. McPhedran became concerned that community resources would prove inadequate to heal the psychological wounds the very existence of the inquiry had surfaced. Unwittingly they had opened a Pandora's box.

The editors of *Psychology Today* believe that the frequency of incidence among lawyers, teachers and clergy falls into the same range as that of the professions they surveyed.

Bringing the Secrets to Light

When we talk about sexual misconduct involving a professional and a client, we are broaching one of the most insidious "family secrets" present in our society. In the past, allegations of such offenses were greeted with denial by the accused. And professional societies consistently acted to protect their members rather than to insure justice for those the professions exist to serve.

Until recently, victims of abuse and their proponents within the professions have been reticent to challenge the professional establishments. Often they were bullied into acquiescence by thoughts of the public shame and humiliation to which speaking out would likely expose them. Such nightmares have repeatedly been confirmed through high-profile incidents in which the courts or ethics committees absolved an accused professional, and the complainants experienced public ostracism. The cost of making an accusation can be severe!

Today, however, the climate is rapidly changing. In recent years an increasing number of people have been willing to risk personal reputation and "go public" with their stories of abuse and victimization. Whether or not Anita Hill's testimony was true, the Hill-Thomas case, which grabbed the headlines 'n the early 1990s, has changed forever the way sexual abuse and harassment are viewed in North America. More and more complainants are unwilling to keep their secrets to themselves, a trend which will accelerate in the future.

The negative effects of burying dark secrets within the hidden recesses of one's psyche has become a major interest of clinical psychologists. Imber Black describes the debilitating effects of untold secrets: "The presence of a central secret in a family or a relationship distorts and mystifies the communication process."[4] It impairs development, frustrates problem solving, engenders shame and produces both guilt and anxiety.[5] Convinced that secrets shape family and therapeutic relationships, psychologists are increasingly realizing that exposing one's secrets is a crucial component in the healing process. Consequently, bringing secrets to light has become not only a legal and ethical issue but a major concern in the treatment of victims of abuse. Clinicians often conclude that if healing cannot take place without debilitating secrets being exposed, then they as professionals are responsible to help clients bring them into the open, regardless of the accompanying consequences.

When practiced without caution, of course, certain techniques, including therapy designed to facilitate recalling long-suppressed experiences of abuse, can lead to misuse and even exploitation. But to the extent that it encourages the truth to emerge, we as Christians ought to applaud the trend toward greater openness. Acknowledging the truth may be difficult, but it can eventually facilitate healing and promote a safer environment for persons who seek professional help. When carried out with integrity, therefore, we can welcome attempts to bring to light a painful past for the sake of healing in the present. The time has indeed come for what was said in the dark to be heard in the daylight and what was whispered in the ear in the inner rooms to be proclaimed from the roofs (Luke 12:3).

Discovering the Exploitation of Power
Contributing to the secretive cloak covering professional sexual misconduct

is a power dynamic often at work in abusive relationships. An important voice in bringing this dimension to light has been the psychologist Peter Rutter. Numerous interviews led him to realize how pervasive sexual misconduct is within his own profession. He began to find it "in places I had never thought to look."[6]

Rutter insists that in our culture the connection to power makes sexual misconduct largely a male problem. Amazed at "how easily well respected men of power could repeatedly sexually exploit women without ever being discovered,"[7] Rutter concludes that this exploitation occurs because a man in power is able to capitalize on a woman's trust, making it difficult for her to say no to sexual contact.

On this basis Rutter challenges us to move beyond the narrow focus of the past and understand sexual misconduct in broad terms. In fact, he asserts that "any behavior by a man in power within what I define as the forbidden zone is inherently exploitive of a woman's trust."[8]

By "the forbidden zone" Rutter means any sexual contact that occurs within professional relationships of trust, such as may be perpetrated by a therapist.[9] Misconduct, therefore, includes any "sexual contact between men in power and women under their care."[10] Rutter explains: "Any physical contact or bodily movement intended to express or arouse erotic interest is 'sexual behavior.' Distinctions as to who touched whom, in what way, or on what part of the body are irrelevant when it comes to sex in the forbidden zone, where any touching with erotic interest, including touching oneself, is a violation of the boundary. Even an ostensibly accidental brushing of a woman's body must be considered sexually invasive when a man has arranged, with erotic interest, to be close enough so that this 'accident' might occur. 'Sexual invasion' can occur even when there is no touching of the other person."[11]

Breaking the Conspiracy of Silence

Although not restricted to men, sexual misconduct on the part of a professional is overwhelmingly perpetrated by men against women, rather than by women against men. In fact, Rutter boldly asserts that 96 percent of sexual exploitation by professionals occurs between a man in power and a woman under his care.[12] Rutter also notes that sexual exploitation occurs "in an atmosphere of enforced silence."[13] This silence is honored not only by the participants but also by others who are aware but unwilling to breach the silence. Rutter's goal is to see that the code of silence is broken.

Although in our day sexual misconduct is overwhelmingly an abuse of male power, it is neither exclusively nor intrinsically so, as Rutter seems to imply. The editors of *Psychology Today* are closer to the truth: "In fact sexual exploitation takes place in all gender combinations, in heterosexual and homosexual varieties."[14] Sexual misconduct is not *inherently* connected to the abuse of male power. Rather, it has *become* a problem of male power, because power remains largely lodged with males in the professions, in our society and certainly in most churches.

In the past the church contributed to the conspiracy of silence that characterized the other caregiving professions. Clergy sexual misconduct was one of those secrets that lurked in the hidden recesses of church life. But so long as the church cajoles the victims to remain silent, it only compounds the problem and augments the damage. Whereas once people were content to deny or ignore this issue, they now will not, cannot and should not dismiss it.

This book seeks to contribute to the task of bringing to light and responding to the epidemic of clergy sexual misconduct for the sake of promoting healing in the lives of the victims and in the life of the church itself.

In the following pages we concern ourselves solely with the phenomenon of *clergy* sexual misconduct involving a *male* pastor and a *female* congregant. We readily acknowledge that this narrow focus does not exhaust the vast variety of misconduct currently present within the church.

We realize that the advent of women's ordination means that clergy sexual misconduct is theoretically no longer an exclusively male offense. Nor do men have a monopoly on sexual failure. However, all available statistics indicate that in the overwhelming majority of cases, males are the perpetrators of sexual misbehavior and abuse. Family violence in North America, for example, is by and large perpetrated by males. One estimate asserts that "98.8% of child sexual abusers are men and that in 95% of the cases of 'spousal' assault, the male is the abuser."[15] What is true in the general population is true in the pastorate, if for no other reason than that men continue to dominate the ordained ministry.[16]

Likewise we realize that contact between a male pastor and a female congregant under his care is not the only form of clergy sexual misconduct. Nevertheless, this phenomenon accounts for the greatest number of incidents, at least in evangelical churches. So it currently looms as the most devastating problem evangelicals must address.

In the subsequent discussion we develop the thesis that clergy sexual misconduct is a grave betrayal of trust. This betrayal operates in two directions. It is a violation of a sacred sexual trust, marring the beautiful picture God has given of the relationship of Christ and the church. And it is a violation of a power trust, abusing the privilege of the pastoral position with which the ordained leader has been endowed by the church and its Lord.

The goal of the discussion is to inform and motivate God's people to take appropriate steps to combat this debilitating phenomenon. We must act against clergy sexual misconduct for the sake of the victims, for the sake of the reputation of the gospel, but above all for the sake of God's glory.

1
The Scope
of the Problem

Sixteen-year-old Sandy found herself attracted to the youth pastor of her church. He seemed to model a dynamic Christianity that was missing in her life. While the two of them were involved in a church mission project, she noticed his special interest in her. Never having had a boyfriend and uninitiated in sexual matters, Sandy was delighted with his physical attentions. Yet she also felt uncomfortable about the situation. Caught between conflicting emotions, she eventually yielded to the pastor's sexual desires, losing her virginity and with it her innocence. It took Sandy twenty-five years before she was able to verbalize the hurt and sense of betrayal this incident caused.

Sandy retained her basic Christian faith and her commitment to the local church. Not every victim of clergy sexual misconduct is able to do so. Referring to the hurt and ostracism she encountered, a woman offered this comment about the title of an article dealing with sexual misconduct, published in a Christian paper: " 'Ministers at Risk'? Everyone is at risk, but more so the victims, because our pain and demise is seldom heard. For me, no one would listen as my soul was stolen and destroyed."[1] She then described her four-year struggle with clergy sexual and spiritual misconduct. Tragically she fell into the hands of a pastor who knew of her past history as a victim of abuse and took advantage of it. She wrote, "I've been shipwrecked by Rev. Abuser's angry and violent abuse of me and a church in denial and control."

At one time pastors basked in the respect and trust not only of congregants but also of the wider community. Ministers were viewed as the epitome of integrity—including sexual integrity. Yet in the past few years the pastorate has become a vocation in free fall. We can hardly open a newspaper, listen to a radio talk show, watch a television program or skim through a magazine without confronting yet another case of clergy sexual misconduct. And the media appear all to willing to give a high profile to stories of the latest sexual failings of prominent ministers. In fact, misconduct has become so wide-spread that many insurance companies are limiting their coverage of abuse cases or excluding it altogether.[2]

How should we deal with the tide of clergy sexual misconduct which has washed on the shores of the church?

The Extent of Misconduct

An issue in Old Testament, church and recent history. Clergy sexual misconduct is not uniquely contemporary; it dates even to biblical times. The Old Testament reports that God rejected the sons of the priest Eli because they misused their position to engage in sexual misconduct. These wicked men, who had "no regard for the LORD" (1 Samuel 2:12), "slept with the women who served at the entrance to the Tent of Meeting" (v. 22).

The early church had occasion to deal with similar difficulties. Perhaps the dangers that sexual misconduct posed to New Testament leaders lay behind Paul's strong statement: "I punish my body and enslave it, so that after proclaiming to others I myself should not be disqualified" (1 Corinthians 9:27 NRSV). The pitfalls of misuse led early church leaders such as Jerome, Tertullian and Augustine to instruct pastors in how to handle their sexuality.

The problem of clergy sexual misconduct is no stranger to church life in North America. Nathaniel Hawthorne's classic novel, *The Scarlet Letter*, focuses on the social ostracism suffered by a woman who was victimized by the young, popular parish pastor. And as we noted earlier, the most influential clergyman of the nineteenth century, Henry Ward Beecher, tainted his reputation by an episode of sexual misconduct.

Until recently, some Christians attempted to relegate clergy sexual misconduct to the era prior to the sexual revolution when prudishness supposedly led to unbridled abuse. But rather than diminishing since the 1960s, the phenomenon stubbornly remains with us. Indeed, beginning in the 1980s, victims of sexual misconduct found a new freedom to expose what had previously been all-too-readily kept secret. In the mid-1980s clergy sexual harassment even made the pages of the *Ladies Home Journal*.[3]

An issue on the rise. Clergy sexual misconduct is not a new phenomenon. Yet several dimensions of the problem are new. It now receives an unprecedented public profile, as victims have become increasingly willing to tell—and the media to disseminate—the excruciating stories of clergy abuse.

This new profile has led us to discover another grave dimension of the phenomenon, namely, its extent. Until recently church and society generally responded with denial to allegations of clergy sexual misconduct. Even in the present era of disclosure, only a small percentage of abuse cases come to the light. A recent study of the Manitoba Branch of the Canadian Mental Health Association discovered that out of 82 cases of professional abuse, only 24 of the victims had reported the situation to police or other professionals. And only four were convinced that their complaints had been taken seriously.[4] Consequently, it is difficult to assess the degree to which abuse is on the rise. Nevertheless, it appears to have hit epidemic proportions.

An issue that is broad in scope. Clergy sexual misconduct comes in many varieties. It may be limited to seemingly innocent sexual harassment directed toward a coworker—whether a woman on the pastoral staff or the church receptionist. It may entail a single extramarital affair, one "fall from grace" when in a moment of severe stress coupled with a "down" time in his marriage the pastor turns to someone he believes is available. Or it could mushroom into involvement with several congregants simultaneously. In extreme cases abuse may develop into an ongoing pattern of conduct, such as was the situation of the man who victimized sixteen-year-old Sandy.

Our list of perpetrators of misconduct could be widened to include the pedophile, the promiscuous homosexual pastor and the voyeur. And acts of sexual failure could include the whole raft of behaviors Masters and Johnson call "paraphilia." But the most devastating and common incidents involve a male pastor and a female congregant. In fact, the incidence of this kind of sexual impropriety among male clergy may exceed the 10 percent estimate for male psychotherapists.[5] This problem now touches many people and many churches.

An issue throughout the clergy. Not only does it include a variety of activities, but clergy sexual misconduct involves pastors in differing life stages and situations. Single or married, young or old, the recently ordained or the pastor of long standing who is thought to be a model for the church and community—any pastor is susceptible to the temptation of misconduct. And such acts are perpetrated by ministers of rural churches as well as urban churches, although it is often the city pastor who is reported.

Clergy sexual misconduct touches churches of all denominations—Roman Catholic, mainline Protestant, evangelical and charismatic.

Today the situation has grown especially acute among Catholics. According to David Rice, "almost one quarter of the active priests in the world" have left the ministry largely for sexual and marital reasons.[6] Richard Sipe maintains that "about 20 percent of priests vowed to celibacy . . . are at one time involved either in a more or less stable sexual relationship with a woman or, alternatively, with sequential women in an identifiable pattern of behavior. An additional 8 to 10 percent of priests are at a stage of heterosexual exploration that often involves incidental sexual contacts." Sipe explains: "The latter is like dating and pre-dating behavior, where no relationship exists, nor any particular pattern of sexual involvement. This behavior can be the limit of the priest's experimentation, or can evolve into a pattern of sexual activity or a relationship."[7] This problem, added to the phenomenon of child sexual abuse among clergy and the intense disagreement over women's ordination, has catapulted matters of sexuality to the forefront of Roman Catholic concern.

But Protestants are not immune. According to officials of the United Church of Canada, the incidence of sexual misconduct by clergy has reached "horrific proportions." The denominational panel on sexual abuse reported that "women are more likely to get sexually harassed in the church than in the workplace" and that "clergy were sexually exploiting their parishioners at twice the rate of secular therapists."[8] In a 1984 survey among three hundred ministers in the United States, 39 percent reported sexual contact and 12.7 percent actual sexual intercourse with a congregant. In addition, 76.5 percent indicated that they knew of a minister who they believed had engaged in sexual intercourse with a congregant.[9] No wonder Karen Lebacqz and Ronald Barton conclude, "Our experience indicates that virtually every denomination in every region in the United States has dealt with or is struggling to deal with some instance of sexual indiscretion or abuse on the part of a pastor."[10]

Nor do evangelicals find that their commitment to biblical norms guarantees a scandal-free church environment. Our naiveté was shaken in the 1980s by a series of revelations of sexual indiscretions involving prominent leaders. In one week we learned of the failures of John Howard Yoder, Graham Pulkingham and David Hocking. The accusations included "sexual misconduct toward eight women who are in positions of national church leadership,"[11] "several homosexual liaisons, some with counselees, over the past two decades,"[12] and "an affair of long standing."[13]

Sexual misconduct does not entrap only well-known personalities. Prominent leaders are but the tip of a menacing iceberg. They represent a whole group of people whose names would not cause a ripple of recognition outside the communities where they live. Twenty-three percent of clergy responding to a 1987 *Christianity Today* survey said that since entering local church ministry they had engaged in some form of sexual behavior they considered inappropriate. Twelve percent admitted to having sexual intercourse with someone other than their spouse.[14] In a more recent survey among pastors serving in Southern Baptist congregations, 6 percent of the respondents admitted that they had had sexual contact with a person currently affiliated with their church, whereas over 4 percent indicated that they had had such contact with a former congregant. More significantly, over 70 percent affirmed knowledge of other ministers who had had sexual contact with a congregant, and over 24 percent had counseled a woman who claimed to have had such contact with a minister.[15] These statistics include only the approximately 30 percent of pastors who were willing to respond to the survey. We can only wonder what story would be told by the other 70 percent who did not!

Such surveys suggest that there is little reason to anticipate any significant difference in behavior between clergy serving the United Church of Canada and those who subscribe to *Christianity Today*. They may espouse different theological understandings and opposing views about the nature of sexuality, but they engage in a similar pattern of sexual failure.

Just as there is a variety of offenses and offenders, so also clergy sexual misconduct is perpetrated against a variety of congregants. It touches young and older women, both single and married. Its victims come from all social classes and backgrounds. They include congregants facing a variety of problems, including bereavement, marital difficulties, past experiences of abuse, family of origin problems, or naiveté over sexual matters. Although every situation of misconduct is distinct, victims often share a troubled background, including being violated by men they believed to be worthy of trust. This background makes them vulnerable to the sexual advances of a seemingly caring man.

The Church's Response to Misconduct

Sonia was in her middle thirties, an attractive woman who was well liked in her local church. What most people did not know was that her outgoing façade hid a history of abuse. When her father consumed too much alcohol, the other side of this normally successful and charming man emerged. He inflicted physical and psychological damage on any family member who dared cross him. Sonia grew up terrorized by him. And as is typical, she then married a man who turned out to be like her father.

One day in desperation Sonia broke the silence and shared the family secrets with her pastor. For the first time in her life she believed she had discovered a relationship that was intimate, warm and engendering of trust. This beautiful man listened to her with great empathy. He was able to understand her, because he came from a similar background.

Imperceptibly, however, Sonia developed an uneasiness with their relationship. She began to wonder if he was attracted to her, for she certainly was attracted to him. Sonia dismissed such thoughts, but they kept recurring. The pastor, in turn, began to share with her his own unhappy marriage. Sonia was flattered by this exchange of intimacy and soon began to fantasize about a sexual relationship with him. When he made the first overt sexual advances, she was more than ready to respond. She rationalized her action by thinking that it was only right for her to make up for the inadequacies of his wife and thereby enhance her pastor's ministry.

Sonia had become a coconspirator in deception and infidelity. But she was also a victim—of her past, her family of origin, her choice of a partner, and the pastor himself. The emotional and spiritual damage the affair inflicted on her would be almost impossible to repair. But that was only the beginning.

Inevitably the pastor's wife discovered the extent of the relationship. They had kept previous affairs from threatening his professional standing. But in this particular case she was not the last person to find out. No longer willing to be victimized by her adulterous husband, she told her story to the man who chaired the church board.

At first the church leaders did everything possible to prevent a public scandal. But the situation proved unmanageable. Now Sonia discovered that the church members did not view her as a victim but as a seductress who had led their beloved pastor astray and had embarrassed the church. She received anonymous phone calls and hate correspondence, and quickly discovered that she was no longer welcome at her church. Not only was Sonia's marriage in tatters and her self-esteem irreparably damaged, but all her sources of emotional and spiritual support had turned against her as well.

Sonia's congregation responded to the act of adultery in a manner typical of how many churches deal with clergy sexual misconduct. In the beginning the leaders sought to preserve the secret. When this failed, they directed their energies to protecting the church's good name and the pastor's reputation. The members of the congregation saddled Sonia with the blame and excused the pastor's conduct with the typical clichés: "After all, even the pastor is human!" "The poor man's wife obviously wasn't able to provide adequately for his sexual needs."

The typical response, however, accomplishes no positive benefit. It fails to assist the pastor in confronting his behavior so that he can own his responsibility for the affair. Often denominational officials join in the conspiracy of silence when they seek ways of placing the pastor in another location without disclosing the reason for the transfer.

Seductive females do lurk in the halls of the church, of course. But there are predatory pastors on the prowl as well. We acknowledge the former too easily but find it difficult to recognize the latter. Rarely do we inquire as to what leads a woman to develop seductive patterns of relating to men. Seldom do we concern ourselves with what happens to the "other woman" once the storm has broken.

Yet we see indications that a change in attitude may be developing. The change is due in part to a new awareness of the problem of sexual misconduct within the helping professions. This change is especially evident among counselors and psychologists, as Herbert Strean notes: "In contrast to the laissez-faire attitude that was shown toward clinicians like Jung, Rank, Ferenczi, and Jones for their sexual improprieties, today's therapists who have sexual liaisons with their patients are subject to lawsuits, loss of their licenses, disbarment from professional organizations, and other retaliatory measures."[16]

Glen Gabbard likens sexual exploitation by a therapist to incest: "Incest victims and those who have been sexually exploited by professionals have remarkably similar symptoms: shame, intense guilt associated with a feeling that they were somehow responsible for their victimization, feelings of isolation and forced silence, poor self-esteem, suicidal and/or self-destructive behavior and denial. Reactions of friends and family—disbelief, discounting, embarrassment—are also similar in both groups."[17]

Gabbard's analogy is especially appropriate to the pastorate. The church is a spiritual family. Consequently, the dynamics of human families—including dysfunctional patterns of behavior—often develop in congregations as well. Viewed from this perspective, clergy sexual misconduct may be likened to spiritual incest. Rather than denying its presence, the family of God must take the lead in dealing with clergy sexual abuse in a healthy, healing manner. Such healing begins as we realize the devastating effects of such misconduct among us.

We cannot calculate the extent of the destructiveness of clergy sexual misconduct. The violation of a congregant is a grave evil that works devastating effects in several directions.[18]

How Misconduct Affects the Pastor

Most obvious are the effects of sexual misconduct on the pastor's own ministry. This evil touches the perpetrator himself.

Once the scandal becomes public, the offending minister faces great loss. Some of these losses are professional. The pastor's reputation and credibility in the church and in the wider society are inevitably diminished, if not destroyed. He may find his position as a minister temporarily or even permanently jeopardized. And he may find himself facing charges of legal liability.

The pastor's losses will likely be personal as well. He may lose his church family, and friends may turn away from him. He faces the potential loss of his own spouse and family. But the most tragic loss lies elsewhere. His act marks the betrayal of his personal call as a pastor.

The experience of grave loss almost inevitably leads the pastor into a sense of guilt and depression.

Generally the paramount desire of the church leadership is to rescue the pastor, or at least minimize the damage to him and the institution he serves. Whether or not the process they initiate is justifiable, they are surely correct that the offending pastor faces the ruin of what may have been a productive and effective ministry.

Pastor Jack was guilty of a sexual indiscretion. Although it had not yet entailed adultery, it was sufficient to shock the church board. Facing public scandal and the possibility of a lawsuit, they gladly accepted the pastor's panic-stricken resignation. The affair resulted in great loss for Jack. Formerly he had been warmly welcomed into any home in the church and had constantly received phone calls of affirmation. In addition, he had been a respected person in the community. But now his phone ceased to ring, and speaking invitations stopped coming. Most excruciating of all, however, he now sensed the open contempt of the community and rejection by his former church members.

At first Jack's wife and family supported him as best they could. But they too had lost their place in the church. After an initial empathic reaction, church members became confused as to how to respond to them. In vain they looked for another church that could provide the support they so desperately needed. So anger replaced the pity they had initially felt for their father and spouse.

In the end Jack lost not only his job but also his sense of vocation, social network, financial security and sense of personal value and worth. His theological convictions led him to believe that he could experience forgiveness from God and others. But he did not have the theological expertise to deal with his shame. He contemplated a very different future with little hope. Jack grew depressed and even flirted with suicide. Never having had deep feelings for the other woman, he became angry at her for what he perceived she did to him and his family.

Jack believed that the church leadership, with whom he had once enjoyed a cordial relationship, mishandled the situation. The fact is, however, they would have preferred to rescue him. Like their pastor, they at first blamed the woman and suspected that Jack's wife did not sufficiently satisfy him. But because his misconduct so quickly became a public scandal, his offer of resignation seemed the easiest and quickest solution to the problem.

Looking back, Jack now realizes that he went from being a loved and esteemed leader to being a pariah. The gains for him were nil, whereas his losses were immense. He knows that the currency of ministry is trust, but his action destroyed this trust.

In *Rebuilding Your Broken World*, Gordon MacDonald writes candidly about the implications of his own failure: "I am a broken-world person because a few years ago I betrayed the covenants of my marriage. For the rest of my life I will have to live with the knowledge that I brought deep sorrow to my wife, to my children, and to friends and others who have trusted me for many years."[19] Whatever assessment befits MacDonald's failure and the rebuilding process that ensued, his description of the "deep sorrow" an affair caused his wife, children, friends and others is no exaggeration.

How Misconduct Affects the Congregation

A pastor's actions never occur in isolation. Instead, they affect a host of other persons. Because of his role as a leader within the Christian community, a minister's involvement in sexual misconduct directly touches his congregation.

When a pastor's affair becomes public knowledge, the church he serves faces great loss. This loss includes certain intangible aspects associated with a congregation's reputation in the wider society. The pastor's action will likely evoke public embarrassment and a diminishing of the church's credibility in the community. It may even entangle the congregation in legal difficulties.

Equally devastating is the internal turmoil that ensues when the congregation learns that their pastor has engaged in sexual misconduct. News of the unfortunate event will inevitably lead to polarization, even strife, within the church membership. Persons who either came to faith in Christ or made significant spiritual or emotional progress as a result of the pastor's ministry will be hurt, confused and embarrassed. They will question the genuineness of what has taken place in their own lives through this flawed individual.

Torn between anger and empathy, the church will experience a divisiveness borne out of confusion. No matter how gross the offense, some members will support the pastor—some for all the wrong reasons. Persons representing all sides of the debate will lose confidence in the church leadership. Regardless of the final outcome, the institution will be damaged, in some cases beyond repair.

Forced to deal with an uncomfortable, debilitating situation, the church will experience a loss of morale both institutionally and individually. The congregation will find itself dissipating its corporate energy, as service and outreach are displaced by the internal crisis as the focus of available resources. For a period of time membership growth will be stymied, as few people join and disgruntled members drop out.

Karen Lebacqz and Ronald Burton rightly conclude that "whenever a pastor is accused of inappropriate sexual conduct within a church, the bonds of trust between that pastor and the congregation are stretched to the breaking point. The focus of attention within the congregation shifts from the worship of God and the mission that flows out of that worship and begins instead to concentrate on the behavior of the pastor and of church members."[20]

How Misconduct Affects the Family

Sexual misconduct is professionally serious. It stands as a denial of all the pastor has claimed to be, has been seen to be and has taught others to be. For this reason it entails grave consequences for the minister himself. It is also institutionally serious, affecting the congregation which he has served. However, the effects of clergy sexual misconduct move beyond the pastor and his congregation. The evil also touches his spouse and family.

Any act of marital infidelity carries consequences for the offending person's spouse. Especially devastating for a faithful wife is the discovery that her husband has engaged in deceit. Annette Lawson expresses the feelings of many wives of adulterous husbands: "It was the deceit I couldn't bear—that he had been carrying on with her for years and I never knew."[21] Another woman offers this heart-wrenching response: "It is impossible to describe the mental and physical pain—if he dies before me, he will have died twice."[22] It is difficult to find words to describe the anger, grief, sense of guilt, shame and disillusionment at the deepest level that result from the infidelity of a person's spouse.[23]

Writing in *Psychology Today*, Frank Pittman describes the results of Howard's disclosure to Harriett and their children that he was leaving them for Maxine:

> Harriett went into a rage and hit him. The children went berserk. The younger daughter cried inconsolably, the older one became bulimic, the son quit school and refused to leave his room. . . . The kids were carrying on so on the telephone, Howard stopped calling them for a few months, not wanting to upset them. Meanwhile he and Maxine, who had left her kids behind as well, borrowed some money from his mother and moved to the coast where they bought into a marina—the only thing they had in common was the pleasure of fishing.[24]

But the trauma that arises from the sexual misconduct of a pastor has additional dimensions. If he is married, his act of indiscretion can be devastating to his wife. Not only does it raise in her mind the typical questions about personal adequacy in matters of sex, it calls into question her adequacy in every aspect of life, including her role as "the pastor's wife." And she can anticipate that people both within and outside the church will raise similar questions.

Regardless of the outcome of the affair for her husband as a professional, she will endure loss of public esteem. But should he lose his ministerial post, she will be denied her position in the church. She may be asked to vacate her home. And should the affair force her husband into a change of profession, she will forfeit her entire way of life.

Often the task of explaining "Daddy's problem" to the children will fall to the pastor's wife. This will come at a time when she may not understand it herself.

The children face losses similar to those confronting their mother. They too will lose face among their church peers. They likely will be cut off from church friends as the family searches for another congregation to join. Should their father's sexual misconduct lead to a divorce, they will undergo the trauma that befalls all children in such situations. In addition they may have to shoulder the effects of their father's loss of employment or change of career.

How Misconduct Affects the Other Woman Involved

Despite the devastating effects of clergy sexual misconduct on the pastor, his church and his family, there is no denying the special devastation suffered by the Sonias of the church world. Generally "the other woman" drops out of the story at the first possible moment. Few people, if any, truly care about her or reach out to her.

Marie Fortune describes this woman as being in "double jeopardy." In truth, hers is often a triple jeopardy. Problems posed by her dysfunctional family of origin initially led her to seek out the pastor's care. Rather than being a source of personal healing, however, the affair was immensely destructive. Once the liaison became public she also found herself rejected and abandoned by her church fellowship. The well-being of this poor woman is jeopardized first by her physical family, then by her pastor's betrayal of her, and finally by the alienation of her spiritual family.

This loss is exemplified in the reaction of a church deacon to the sexual misbehavior of his highly respected pastor. The deacon became indignant when he discovered that although the pastor had stumbled in a similar manner in a previous pastorate, his former congregation had never disclosed this information. But the deacon's harshest comments were reserved for the congregant with whom the minister had been involved. He was mystified that she would seek to remain a part of the congregation: "She actually turned up in church last Sunday morning. We will have to speak to her about that."

In certain ways, the effects of clergy sexual misconduct on the "other woman" parallel those experienced by victims of practitioners in the other caregiving professions.

The Ontario College of Physicians, for example, concludes that sexual abuse by a medical doctor may lead to physical effects. These include skeletal and muscle problems, back pain, nervous symptoms such as difficulty breathing and gastrointestinal disorders, and changes in appetite. Misconduct may likewise bring psychological effects, such as intense anxiety, fear, panic, depression, self-mutilation, suicidal thoughts or behaviors, mood or attitude changes, guilt, anger, loss of trust in the world and society. Many victims also lose their ability to trust doctors and health-care providers.[25] The patient's social well-being may also be affected. She may experience difficulty developing or maintaining intimate relationships, she may withdraw socially and she may even begin to abuse alcohol or drugs.[26] Clergy sexual misconduct can give rise to similar effects.

In addition to mirroring these effects, sexual misconduct by a therapist can cause grave damage to a victim's view of herself as a woman. When led into a sexual liaison by a trusted caregiver, a woman senses that she has been manipulated, violated and used. Rutter notes the potential devastation: "How a woman is treated in relationships of trust can make the difference between whether she experiences her femininity as a force to be valued and respected or as a commodity to be exploited."[27]

The problem is compounded when the woman has come to the caregiver for assistance in healing former hurts, especially those incurred from an earlier abusive relationship with a trusted professional. Janice Russell offers this chilling appraisal: "The available research suggests that more than one half of practising therapists will work with a client who has experienced sexual intimacy/exploitation with a previous therapist."[28]

When the perpetrator of sexual misconduct is a woman's pastor, the devastation to her self-image is even more acute. Pamela Cooper-White states the problem succinctly:

> The pastoral relationship can and should be a sacred trust, a place where a parishioner can come with the deepest wounds and vulnerabilities— where she can even act out sexually. By modeling appropriate boundaries and healthy responses, the pastor can begin to empower her to heal those wounds. The harm done when this is exploited is no less than a violation of sacred space, which further ruptures and destroys the woman's boundaries, devastating her mental health and her sense of self.[29]

The effects of clergy sexual misconduct extend beyond the victim's sense of self. The woman will likely suffer guilt, as she blames herself for the sexual liaison. During the ensuing trauma she may experience wide shifts in emotion. From a sense of emptiness and isolation, her mood could deepen into desperation, suppressed rage and finally even suicidal feelings.

As a result of an incident of clergy sexual misconduct a woman may struggle indefinitely with what psychologists call posttraumatic stress disorder.[30] The victim relives the event over and over in the form of flashbacks. The ongoing stress these flashbacks cause may become evident in bouts of insomnia, irritability and loss of concentration. In the end, the victim's life may even become absorbed by the reoccurring flashbacks.

However difficult, the physical and psychological traumas arising from clergy sexual misconduct pale in comparison to its potential spiritual effects. The woman's sense of shame, self-blame and guilt may lead to a feeling of estrangement. As members of her congregation reject her, she may come to believe that she was betrayed not only by her pastor but also by her church, even by her God. Her ensuing crisis of faith may ultimately lead to a bitter end. The woman may be tempted to discard her earlier, and perhaps lifelong, religious commitment.

In commenting on the case of Peter Donovan, Marie Fortune describes the loss of faith that often results:

> Donovan had access to the women's deepest and truest selves. The women looked to him not only as counselor, but as spiritual guide and protector. The psychological pain he caused was magnified and took on cosmic proportions. Not only were the women betrayed by a trusted professional, but they were betrayed by one who professed to represent God: Hence they felt betrayed by God as well.

As a result, "the foundations of their relationships with God were shaken."[31]

How Misconduct Affects the Gospel

Clergy sexual misconduct carries grave consequences for the pastor, the church, his spouse and the woman involved in the affair. The greatest tragedy, however, lies in its debilitating effects for the gospel. Each act of clergy indiscretion marks a violation of the Christian message and its credibility.

A pastor who enters into an illicit sexual relationship reinforces the disbelief, even cynicism, of the unbelieving world. Skeptics correctly wonder how a Christian leader can honestly commend the gospel to others when his own conduct displays no higher standard of sexual morality than that of those he sees as needing the salvation message.

Not only does the guilty pastor belie the gospel he proclaims, but above all he tarnishes the reputation of the Christ he represents. Rather than hallowing the holy name of our Lord, rather than causing God's name to be well thought of in the world, he has brought reproach on the One he claims to serve. His action means that the church is no longer a safe haven for wounded persons in search of healing. Instead, what our Lord intends as a refuge has become a place of potential injury.

Clergy sexual misconduct entails a wrong committed on several fronts. Apart from being a transgression of biblical sexual norms, it is a violation of a covenant made with many persons—the pastor's spouse and family, the congregant against whom he perpetrated the act, the congregation that he serves and the church as a whole. But above all, misconduct involves a betrayal of a vow with God which the pastor declared at ordination.

Misconduct and the Church

In the light of these effects of clergy sexual misconduct, it is hardly surprising that church bodies and parachurch organizations are frantically working at codes of ethics for leaders and processes for disciplining the wayward. The questions the phenomenon of sexual abuse raises for the Christian community, however, cannot be answered merely by a list of rules and procedures. We are being forced to face hard issues about ourselves, our understanding of Christian leadership and our vision for ministry.

The rise of clergy sexual misconduct calls us to join together in seeking answers to a host of questions:

How could the leaders of a body that sets such high standards be guilty of such appalling behavior?

If the gospel is not powerful enough to prevent leaders from engaging in this kind of misconduct, how can it say anything of significance to the rest of society?

If the incidence of misconduct is indeed higher than that found in other helping professions, what aspects of the professional Christian ministry might lie at the root of the problem?

If the forgotten victims are the congregants who come to the pastor for help, why is so little attention paid to these women?

If clergy misconduct entails a betrayal of trust—a violation of power and of human sexuality, what measures is the church putting into place to protect people from such offenses?

If pastors are so vulnerable, what ethical codes, structures of support and systems of accountability should the church put in place?

What kind of seminary admission procedures and training programs will enable future pastors to avoid the trap of overstepping "the forbidden zone" in their relationships with women?

What rethinking must church leaders engage in, in order to respond adequately to the call for restructuring the pastoral care of women?

Who supports the pastor's wife and children when he has fallen sexually?

What rehabilitation procedures does the phenomenon of clergy sexual misconduct call for? And who is responsible to devise, enforce and engage in it?

What steps can the local church, denomination or parachurch organization take in order to make restitution morally, legally and spiritually to those who have been victimized by their leaders? How can Christian bodies protect themselves from a victimizer without violating the victims or becoming victims themselves?

Many of these questions are new. All of them are troubling. None of them promises easy answers. But the scope of the problem, arising as it does out of a deeply wounded society, demands that we address these issues squarely.

The problems introduced by the epidemic of clergy sexual misconduct are not likely to go away in the near future. On the contrary, the phenomenon appears to have reached such proportions that it could undermine the public perception of the church in the immediate, if not the long term. If the issues clergy sexual misconduct poses are not adequately addressed, and if the problem is not remedied, increasing incidents of abuse may destroy the church in a single generation.

Left unbridled, the sexual misconduct perpetrated by pastors will leave the faithful disillusioned and the skepticism of critics confirmed. It will stop the ears, dull the conscience, silence the Spirit, and from the human perspective make the death of Christ irrelevant. We dare not allow this to happen!

2
The Pastor
at Risk

P astor Steve seemed to embody all the qualities of the ideal Christian leader. When ministering to his congregants, he was warm, genuine and perceptive. Naturally gregarious, Steve had gained the admiration of people in the community as well. Therefore, when a female church member accused him of fondling her, the congregation naturally assumed that she had been fantasizing or perhaps had misinterpreted his behavior.

As the woman's accusation was being rejected, however, warning bells began to ring in the minds of the more discerning church leaders. Could Steve have a problem? The hugs he indiscriminately bestowed were more generous when the recipient was an attractive female. And several women had complained that his actions went beyond mere brotherly affection.

Unfortunately, however, nobody wanted to challenge Steve. Had the leaders investigated the matter, they might have spared the church the disillusionment that emerged when they discovered that Steve had become involved with a number of women both in the congregation and in the community.

What went wrong with Steve? Did he have no inkling that his misconduct would inevitably come to light? Had he no sense of the heavy toll his actions would extract from his wife and family, the victims of his advances, the church he served, let alone the reputation of Christ in the community? Even if his moral compass was malfunctioning, didn't he care about himself? Was he not able to realize that he could lose everything he valued?

Adventist minister Roger Bryant describes the results of his sexual misconduct in an article bearing the stark title "I Committed Adultery."[1] Although he knew there would be fallout from his action, the consequences he anticipated "paled in comparison with experiencing the reality of what happened." In the wake of destroying his family and devastating his children, Bryant experienced an excruciating self-loathing that led to depression and suicidal feelings. He was shunned by church members; even the "official greeter" refused to shake his hand. Not only did the congregation terminate his position, they dropped his church membership without even advising him by telephone. Once a prominent leader in his denomination, he suddenly "ceased to exist," as if he had dropped off the face of the earth. Bryant concludes: "Any one of these consequences of my sin would make for a major life crisis. Put them all together, and my stress load was crushing beyond belief."[2]

The experience Bryant recounts is by no means unusual. Across the theological and denominational spectrum, clergy who have transgressed relate grim stories of rejection, abandonment, guilt, shame and anger. The narratives vary: a Catholic priest leaves the church to marry the woman with whom he has had a relationship for two years, or an evangelical pastor engages in adultery with a counselee. Despite the differing scenarios, the ramifications are always similar. A former student described to us what happened when a congregation discovered that their much loved senior pastor was involved in a compromising relationship with a woman he was counseling: "He never even came back to his office in the church to pick up his personal belongings."

The consequences of clergy sexual misconduct are so enormous it seems inconceivable that any pastor worthy of the name could betray himself and others in this manner. Yet the problem keeps growing. Why? Why does a person indulge in behavior that may give momentary excitement but eventually reaps a whirlwind? What leads a pastor to engage in conduct for which the gains are so few and the losses cataclysmic? What occurs inside the minister who commits a sexual offense? And above all, who—what kind of pastor—is at risk of falling into misconduct?

Who Is Susceptible?

Clergy sexual misconduct knows no theological or ecclesiastical boundaries. The perpetrators come from all denominations and espouse a spectrum of viewpoints. No pastor dare claim that he is immune from temptation merely because of the orthodoxy of his theology or the structure of church he serves.

Clergy sexual misconduct takes many forms, including exhibitionism, voyeurism, child molestation, incest, homosexual promiscuity, and rape. In fact, ministers are exempted from no type of aberrant sexual behavior. Often a pastor finds himself waging a long, lonely battle against the temptation to engage in conduct he knows is unacceptable and dangerous. Sometimes, however, a minister not only loses the battle but even draws the church into his destructive conduct as the congregation becomes the source for the victims of his self-gratification.

Misconduct may be limited to practices which our society finds quite innocent and acceptable. These include a host of acts or statements that convey erotic interest or that are intended to express or arouse interest. Sometimes clergy misconduct takes the form of sexual harassment—actions through which a pastor uses his power over a congregant in order to manipulate or control their relationship for his own ends. Sexual misconduct is especially devastating, however, when it leads to actual sexual relations. The most pervasive and destructive activities involve a male pastor and a female congregant. This is "sex in the forbidden zone," to use Peter Rutter's powerful imagery.[3]

But what type of pastor becomes involved? Who is at risk of perpetrating an inappropriate sexual liaison with a church member?

Some observers of the phenomenon differentiate as many as seven profiles of vulnerable pastors.[4] But Marie Fortune's simple distinction between *predators* and *wanderers* is perhaps more helpful. To these two we would add a third type—the *lover*.

The Predator

The pastor who actively seeks opportunities to abuse women sexually with apparently little or no sense of appropriate personal moral restrictions can be called a *predator*. Masquerading as a concerned pastor, the predator uses his power and position to coerce or manipulate, cloaking his intentions with his ministerial position. He deliberately moves beyond the boundaries of propriety and takes his victims with him. In targeting his victims he is not opposed to using violence if necessary.

Many predators are repeat offenders, having a string of conquests over a long period of time or even being involved with several women simultaneously. The predator's actions may be motivated by unmet sexual or power needs or internal problems he has never adequately faced.

Fortune notes that the pastoral sex offender does not differ significantly from his nonclergy counterpart:

> He is manipulative, coercive, controlling, predatory, and sometimes violent. He may also be charming, bright, competent, and charismatic. He is attracted to powerlessness and vulnerability. He is not psychotic, but is usually sociopathic; that is, he has little or no sense of conscience about his offending behaviors. He usually will minimize, lie, and deny when confronted. For these offenders, the ministry presents an ideal opportunity for access to possible victims of all ages.[5]

The paradigmatic example of a predator is "Peter Donovan," the pastor whose story Fortune brings to light in her book *Is Nothing Sacred?* Fortune draws a similarity between Donovan and incest offenders. Like them, he "played on the loyalty and ambivalence of his victims and extracted their promise of keeping 'our special secret.' "[6]

The Wanderer

In contrast to the predator, the *wanderer* is generally not a violent offender. Nor is he premeditative in his actions. Under normal circumstances he would never contemplate a sexual liaison with a congregant. However, an overwhelming crisis or a major transition in his life may tip the balance, leading him to step over the boundary into the forbidden zone.

The wanderer is generally less successful personally and professionally than the predator. Others may even view him as somewhat inadequate. According to Fortune, the wanderer "has difficulty maintaining boundaries in relationships, and attempts to meet private needs in public arenas."[7] Because he is a vulnerable and inadequate person, the wanderer is "at great risk to become emotionally and sexually involved with a parishioner or counselee."[8] He falls into sexual misconduct through contact with an equally needy woman who "holds the pastor in total positive regard to the point of adoration."[9]

Having observed several of his colleagues shipwreck their ministry through a sexual indiscretion, Pastor Paul determined this would never happen to him. He maintained open communication with his wife, whom he dearly loved. He was disciplined in his relationship with other women, even though he did counsel female congregants when the need arose.

Paul did not receive acclamation for his untiring labors. One woman in the congregation, however, did consistently affirm him. She had unexpectedly lost her husband, but had recovered from her bereavement. Ministering to a difficult congregation located in a small town some distance from their families and friends, Paul and his wife soon viewed this woman as their closest friend.

The crisis came when her mother's illness necessitated that Paul's wife make repeated trips home, sometimes for as long as two weeks. Naturally their mutual friend would drop in on Paul regularly. Also understandable was the deepening intimacy that grew between them.

During one visit the woman gave her pastor a hug to reassure and comfort him as he faced a difficult time in the church. This act, however, broke the dam that they had carefully built and swept away their inhibitions, leading to a single occurrence of sexual intercourse. After the passion subsided, the negative emotions surfaced—shame, guilt, anxiety, feelings of betrayal and blame. They swore each other to secrecy.

On the surface everything continued as usual. There was no scandal. The marriage remained intact. But a triangle had been forged, boundaries had been inappropriately breached, trust had been violated. The secret would cast its shadow over the marriage and the friendship.

Paul wandered only once. Yet his act continued to extract its toll. The spiritual and emotional losses inevitably diminished Paul's already mediocre capacity for ministry.

What went wrong? Pastor Paul's downward spiral into misconduct began with loneliness. Cameron Lee and Jack Balswick see loneliness as a major problem for the pastor and his wife, even in the best of situations. The demands of the ministry often prevent them from finding close friends outside the congregation, while their understanding of their role inhibits them from establishing intimate friendships within the congregation. Consequently, the minister and his wife may share "a common problem of loneliness."[10] Pastor Paul engaged in adultery with the hope of assuaging his loneliness. Ironically, the act only exacerbated the problem. His sense of loneliness increased as he became estranged from his wife and his friend. As a result he became a poorer husband, father, pastor and friend.

The distinction between the predator and the wanderer provides insight into the personality of the offender. But the two types of ministers not only enter the forbidden zone for different reasons, they also respond to detection differently. The predator will generally use all the means in his power to destroy those who bring accusations against him or those who support his accusers. The wanderer, in contrast, is unlikely to mount an effort to protect himself, nor does he have the skills to induce many in his church to support him.

Of the two, the predator is more dangerous and destructive. But whether perpetrated by predator or wanderer, every case of clergy sexual misconduct has the same potential. A sexual liaison between a pastor and a congregant can create havoc for the minister, deeply wound his victim, his church and his family, and defame the gospel in the wider community.

The Lover

In addition to the predator and the wanderer, another type of minister enters the forbidden zone with a congregant. Like them, he transgresses the boundaries of sexual propriety. But he is motivated neither by the thrill of conquest nor by the need to overcome felt personal inadequacies. Rather, this pastor senses that he is in love, and the recipient of his affections happens to be a member of his congregation.

Karen Lebacqz and Ronald Barton offer a helpful description of the situation: "This pastor knows that developing a sexual relationship with a parishioner is suspect and tries diligently to guard against any inappropriate behavior. But this pastor falls in love. And sometimes . . . the pastor marries the parishioner."[11] The two authors call this individual the "normal neurotic." We would simply designate him "the lover."

The fact that occasionally a pastor becomes a lover in relationship to a woman in his congregation raises a thorny question: Is all sexual contact between pastor and congregant problematic? Is it permissible for a minister to become a lover?

Perhaps a pastor can never engage in sexual contact with a congregant, regardless of the situation or of his feelings for her. Maybe, as Peter Rutter maintains, the minister-congregant relationship is a forbidden zone in which sexual contact will always be exploitative and therefore a violation of trust.[12]

Then again, perhaps any absolute ban on romantic contact is too strict. Maybe we should hold out the possibility that a valid interest could develop between a pastor and a congregant which could include mutual consent to sexual intimacy. We cannot deny that pastors date and eventually marry congregants. But under what circumstances would such a relationship avoid the problems outlined earlier?

As Rutter and others note, the pastor-congregant relationship is most susceptible to abuse when it arises in a counseling situation. Since this often is the case, many professionals today are calling for strict guidelines governing any romantic involvement between a counselor and a client. Janice Russell, for example, says that when a romantic interest develops, the therapist should immediately transfer the client to another therapist. Because "the situation and role differential" between counselor and counselee may have triggered the original attraction, Russell argues that the initiative in making social contact must rest with the former client; this principle "gives the client the prerogative of changing his or her mind and not feeling pressured, and allows the client to gain control of the situation." Russell suggests that a useful time gap, such as a minimum of six months, between termination of counseling and such social contact would allow for "cooling off and re-evaluation of the feelings and issues which are pertinent to the situation."[13]

Russell's position finds echo in the British Association for Counselling's *Code of Ethics and Practice for Counsellors* (1990):

Counsellors must not exploit clients financially, sexually, emotionally or in any other way. Engaging in sexual activity with current clients within 12 weeks of the end of the counselling relationship is unethical. If the counselling relationship has been over an extended period of time or been working in-depth a much longer "cooling off" period is required and a lifetime prohibition on a future sexual relationship with the client may be more appropriate.[14]

When a male pastor and a female congregant enter into a counseling relationship, the potential for abuse is significant. The level of vulnerability is less pronounced in those wider aspects of ministry in which congregant and pastor worship and work together within the common church life. In such situations a minister and a church member might well be drawn to each other. They could conceivably develop a healthy relationship in which the pastor's behavior remains ethically upright by professional standards.

While such situations are theoretically possible, as Karen Lebacqz and Ronald Barton rightly conclude, "any attempt at ethical pastor-parishioner sexual contact is fraught with dangers."[15] The potential for abuse, which we explore in chapter four, is unavoidably present within such a relationship.

Further, a pastor who dates a congregant has irrevocably ceased to be her pastor. Should their romantic relationship end, they will never be able to assume their former minister-congregant roles. Lebacqz and Barton explain: "When a pastor begins a dating relationship with a parishioner, the pastoral relationship has been, willy-nilly, relegated to second place behind the potential of the dating relationship. The parishioner has lost her or his pastor. She or he cannot regain that pastoral relationship when the dating ceases, and therefore, in need of a pastor, will move to another parish."[16]

But even viewed solely in practical terms, problems abound because the dating relationship is different for a pastor and a congregant than for two laypeople. A pastor-congregant couple will likely find themselves confronted by difficulties beyond what other dating people face. They may discover that other congregants are jealous of their relationship. The jealousy may arise from other women who would like to date the pastor. Or it may come from members who sense that the relationship is stealing the attention of their minister from his pastoral duties. In addition, the couple may feel a subtle pressure from members of the congregation to marry. Such pressure may move them into a premature marriage or dissuade them from breaking off the relationship even though it has ended.

There is no stereotypical perpetrator of sexual misconduct. Often the offending pastor is a repeat offender who moves from conquest to conquest, leaving a trail of victims in the wake of his exploits. Sometimes the minister is a faithful servant of God whose weakness emerges in the crucible of ministry, and as a result he yields to temptation. Occasionally the minister finds himself romantically drawn to a congregant, and in his passion he becomes her lover.

But what actual factors dispose a pastor—whether predator, wanderer or lover—to become sexually involved with a congregant?

What Causes Sexual Misconduct?

Jim was a committed pastor, a man of convictions. Having entered the ministry out of a profound sense of call, he was always prepared to make whatever sacrifice he deemed necessary to serve the Lord, his congregation and the secular community around him. But Jim struggled with a debilitating problem—pornography. He excused it and at times resisted it. But like a monster, it fed his fantasies. As a result, he found his wife less and less attractive and his marriage increasingly unfulfilling. Jim and his wife had never handled conflict well, but her discovery of his addiction marked the psychological end of the marriage.

Jim found many people to blame for what then happened. His father had been emotionally cold and legalistic. His wife was no longer capable of supporting him as she once had. And the workaholic approach to ministry he had gained from the evangelical seminary he attended was now leading him to burn out. In the end, his dysfunctional family of origin, his growing dissatisfaction with his marriage, the pornography that fed his fantasy life, his capacity for rationalizing his actions, and his oppressive workload combined to set him up for a fall. Jim made sexual advances to a church member who had come to him for counseling.

What led Jim, a dedicated pastor, to become a perpetrator of sexual misconduct? What factors lead any pastor to enter into a sexual liaison with a congregant? Pamela Cooper-White points to the internal dynamics of the pastor himself, which may include

> an abusive childhood; low self-esteem and a fear of failure; deeply held traditional values about male and female roles, however disguised in liberal rhetoric; poor impulse control; a sense of entitlement, of being "above the law," or other narcissistic traits; difficulty accepting responsibility for mistakes and difficulty establishing appropriate intimate relationships and friendships with male peers.[17]

In every situation a variety of forces are likely at work. Taken individually, none may be sufficient to trigger clergy sexual misconduct. But together any number of them can lead an otherwise dedicated pastor into the forbidden zone.[18]

Family Dysfunction

In enumerating the characteristics of the pastor who is prone to sexual failure the contribution of his family context forms the obvious starting point.

Fear of intimacy. When a pastor goes astray, the first response from observers is to raise questions about his marriage, and particularly about his wife. Church people often readily assume that she was simply not providing the kind of family environment that could sustain their pastor through the difficulties he faced in his ministry.

Such accusations may be only half true. The pastor's marriage and family life may have been less than adequate. A lack of marital intimacy and dissatisfaction with marital sex are sometimes factors that contribute to clergy sexual misconduct.[19] But the problem likely runs deeper than the attitude and actions of his wife.

The pastor himself may be largely responsible. He may be caught in what M. F. Schwartz calls a "fear-of-intimacy cycle." This cycle operates when a person is afraid to be intimate with his "intimacy sources" (his wife, for example) and turns instead to persons or things that provide a temporary sense of intimacy (pornography, prostitutes, short affairs with other women). But in the end such conduct only leaves him feeling empty, lonely, ashamed and guilty.[20]

Unrealistic expectations of marriage. The pastor could be suffering disappointment resulting from unmet desires for his marriage. In an era in which society places both high companionship expectations and great strain on marriage, ministers—like others—may enter the marital bond with unrealistic anticipations. Perhaps the most destructive of these is the assumption that being married will meet all his present and future, acknowledged and unknown needs. This assumption sets up the marriage partners for disappointment and failure.

When the pastor-husband discovers that marriage is not the heaven he expected, he may blame his spouse. In so doing he avoids dealing with his own unresolved internal problems, while adding tension to his relationship with his wife. The dynamic of the pastorate only fuels the problem. Even the most inadequate minister attracts people in the congregation who think he is "wonderful." Meanwhile his marriage partner has discovered his shortcomings. No pastor can long fail to notice the discrepancy between his wife's realistic appraisal of him as a husband and the lavish praise that fawning congregants shower on him as "the godly minister." When this occurs, the pastor is vulnerable to the temptation to transfer intimacy from his spouse to those who so uncritically feed his emotional needs.

If an equally needy woman in the congregation comes to the pastor for counseling, the final ingredient for disaster is set in place. A counseling relationship devoid of safeguards or supervision provides the opportunity for two emotionally hungry persons to develop an unhealthy intimacy. Left unchecked, this situation is a sure-fire formula for a fall. As the two find themselves drawn to each other, their intimacy easily takes on an increasingly sexual dimension. Then they might engage in sexual behavior, which in turn usually leads to duplicity, deception, betrayal and eventually disillusionment.

Learned attitudes and addictions. The pattern of relating to others that surfaces in the crucible of marriage and ministry rarely originates in adulthood. It is generally imprinted through a series of experiences during early childhood and set during adolescence. The problems a pastor takes into marriage and ministry, therefore, may in part be the outworking of a dysfunctional family of origin. They may be the product of the "sour grapes" he inherited from his parents.

A dysfunctional family of origin may mean that a pastor carries unresolved childhood issues throughout life. Perhaps his parents were distant and unavailable.[21] Perhaps they failed to assist him in developing a healthy attitude toward his sexuality. They may not have acted as positive role models of healthy male-female relationships. Or they may have simply avoided the topic of sex during the formative period in his life. In a survey conducted by *Leadership* magazine, 76 percent of pastors indicated that sexual issues were never discussed in the home.[22]

Or the minister may suffer the ill effects of addiction in the family. According to Thoburn and Balswick, a history of addiction "leaves a pastor essentially addicted to reaching for emotional highs, such as those experienced in infatuation."[23] As a result, the pastor may be caught up in compulsive behavior, ranging from pornography to serial affairs. And he may feel unable to control his sexual activity.

Low self-esteem and the need for approval. The residue of a dysfunctional family of origin is most evident in the emotional scars—especially the low self-esteem or lack of self-worth—it creases on the brow of its offspring. These scars produce a lingering need for the attention, affection and approval denied in childhood. In fact, the quest for acceptance may be what originally draws some people to the pastorate.

These powerful unmet needs readily pervade every area of life. They affect how a pastor from a dysfunctional background deals with conflict, both in the church and in his personal and family life. Dependent on the approval of others, he may shy away from any difficulty that will call his sense of acceptance into question. He may be reticent to tackle any issue that will not be popular. And he may seek to do whatever is necessary to "keep everybody happy."

The pastor who is driven by unmet emotional needs may be blinded to his own motivation. Thinking he is solely concerned for what will bring praise and honor to the Lord, he may actually make decisions on the basis of what makes him feel accepted, acknowledged and appreciated.

Unfortunately for the pastor, the very needs he unconsciously seeks so diligently cannot be met in the church context. Ministry often repays the minister with everything but the affection, attention and approval he so desperately desires. The ensuing frustration can lead to failure.

The pastor's need for acceptance will likewise affect how he handles intimacy and how he views his own sexuality. When a sense of failure and a low self-image collide, the pastor becomes a prime candidate for seeking approval in all the wrong places, including the arms of a needy woman in his congregation.

In short, all the "big ticket items" of emotional functioning arise from the family in which the person was raised. Like others in society, many ministers suffer from unmet needs arising from a negative message encoded on their psyche in childhood. The pastor who does not acknowledge and deal with the "compact disc" playing in his head will spend his entire life looking to satisfy his insatiable desire for approval. Such a person is vulnerable to the temptation to enter the forbidden zone, hoping thereby to attain the goal of his emotional quest.

Thoburn and Balswick summarize the relationship between unmet emotional needs and susceptibility to sexual misconduct:

Low self-esteem creates a climate for the development of a pseudo-self, hiding the real, fragile, and vulnerable self beneath a pseudo-competent air of virility and conquest. . . . An inability to trust out of fear of rejection, or feelings of shame often leave pastors isolated and lonely; isolated loneliness is often the precursor to clinical depression. Obsessive thoughts about sex or fantasies about having extramarital sex may be ways to mask feelings of depression.[24]

Codependency and the desire to rescue. In addition to instilling a gnawing need for affection, attention and approval, a dysfunctional family of origin may affect the pastor in another way. He may have gained from his upbringing a codependency that colors his manner of relating to others; he becomes a rescuer.

Robert Hemfelt, Frank Minirth and Paul Meier describe the situation: "There are two kinds of people who enter the caring services such as medicine, law enforcement, clergy, counseling and social work: those who are called by God and conscience to the work, and those who are driven by the hidden whip of codependency."[25] Children who grow up in a dysfunctional family marked by "rescuing and enabling," they assert, "will be drawn like magnets to the rescuing professions."[26]

Being a codependent professional, however, carries a liability. It may lead to the overwork and overinvolvement that characterize many pastors. Hemfelt, Minirth and Meier describe the situation: "The rescuer, encouraged to noble sacrifice at every hand, can struggle and work, care always about others, never be selfish. The rescuer is praised for rescuing."[27] But the downside of this is that rescuers never take a good look at what is going on inside their own lives. According to Hemfelt, Minirth and Meier, the rescuer in effect is saying, " 'By keeping my focus firmly on others I need not look, let alone focus, upon myself and my needs.' Unmet needs, denial, pain—in short, the personal things that are unpleasant to deal with—get buried. Unfortunately, they do not fade. They fester."[28]

The codependent rescuer pastor is a prime candidate for clergy sexual misconduct. He needs to solve every problem, fix every fissure and heal every wound. When confronted by a hurting wounded woman, his own need to rescue her will tempt him to move the intimacy of their pastor-congregant relationship into the sexual realm. "What this dear woman needs," he may conclude, "is a loving man." And who can better meet this deep need of the female congregant than the gallant pastor!

Family-of-origin considerations assist us in moving beyond the specific instance of clergy sexual misconduct to view the underlying problems that must be resolved if true healing is to occur.

The situation of Pastor Steve provides a lucid example. His life and ministry were on a slide long before he engaged in sexual relations with women in the church. Although his sexual misconduct was understandably the focus of attention when the news of his activities became public, it was not the root problem that he and his congregation needed to resolve. Steve had become a sexual predator who used his position to indulge himself sexually regardless of the cost to himself and others. Many factors, some dating to his childhood, contributed to his sad state. Unless he is able to face these matters, he is likely to repeat the offense in his next ministerial context.

The family-systems model helps us understand the factors in a pastor's family of origin and in his immediate family that contribute to involvement in sexual misconduct. Edwin H. Friedman finds yet an additional use for the model. He suggests that a defect in the congregation—viewed as an extended family—lies at the basis of clergy burnout.[29] On the basis of his model we might conclude that the pastor who falls (whom Friedman labels "the identified burnout") is to some extent a victim of the system.

Of course, Friedman does not completely abandon the idea of personal responsibility. He acknowledges that the pastor's conduct contributes to the system. But Friedman points out that to focus exclusively on the pastor's sexual transgression is to overlook the crucial role played by the dysfunctional church family and thereby to leave the system untouched. "Certainly, each family member in any system must take responsibility for his or her own behavior," explains Friedman, "but to try to understand problems only in terms of their personality exonerates the system." By so doing, the congregation too readily shifts all responsibility to the pastor they have victimized. In his words, "Worse than that, it increases the burden and the guilt of the symptom bearer."[30]

Although Friedman's position risks removing responsibility from the pastor, it does deserve serious consideration. His view reminds us that no incident of sexual misconduct occurs in isolation. Rather, wider social dynamics are always at work. Not the least of these are our cultural understandings of the meaning and place of sexuality in human life and the differing male and female understandings of sexuality inculturated in us from childhood. We focus more closely on this aspect in chapter three.

The phenomenon of clergy sexual misconduct is symptomatic of deeper social realities. These include understandings of sexuality and power, expectations of clergy, and institutional pressures present in all churches. For this reason, in an attempt to discover what puts a pastor at risk, we must look at the pastorate itself.

The Nature of Pastoral Ministry

Why has a situation that seems so unthinkable—a sexual liaison involving a pastor and a congregant—become such a common phenomenon? Part of the answer to this question lies in the nature of the ministry. There are dynamics at work in the contemporary understanding of the pastorate which invite the intrusion of the sexual dimension of human existence.

The intimacy of shared work. One aspect of this dynamic is the nature and power of sexual attraction itself. As Rutter points out, when two people work together in a context where familiarity and trust develop, they may experience closeness, comfort and a sense of completeness in each other's presence.

Because sexual intercourse is a symbol for our deepest intimacy, a deepening sense of intimacy with another can arouse sexual desire.[31]

The pastoral ministry provides a context in which men and women can work together on projects that, because of their religious connection, lie close to the heart of each participant. The intimacy that arises from participating in a common, heartfelt cause can serve as a catalyst for the development of a sexual attraction between a pastor and a female colleague or coworker.

In the person of the pastor, the inherent power of sexual attraction is coupled with a second aspect, the power of the clergy office. His various roles within the congregation open the way for a pastor to become a focus for the intense feelings of congregants.[32]

Emotional transference. The feelings of church members can be triggered by the pastor's role as worship leader and spiritual teacher. Many contemporary churches are abandoning the sterility of past modes of worship and rediscovering the importance of the senses in the worship context. As a result congregants are finding worship to be an uplifting emotional experience. In addition to functioning as worship leader, the pastor fulfills the role of spiritual teacher, the one who seeks to awaken in congregants a yearning for God. Personal spiritual awakening and the experience of worship release passionate feelings that church members seek to direct toward God. However, they may unconsciously focus their feelings on someone who in their understanding represents God—the pastor.[33]

The feelings of a church member may also be triggered by the role of the minister as pastoral caregiver. According to Don S. Browning, pastoral care has two principal functions, "the incorporation of members and their discipline in the group goals and practices of the church" and "the assistance of persons in handling certain crises and conflicts having to do with existential, developmental, interpersonal, and social strains."[34] The pastoral care role, especially its second, ongoing aspect, brings pastor and congregant together in a bonding relationship.

Through the course of his ministry within a congregation, a pastor may become the only person to whom many church members have shared the intimate details of their personal life histories. In this manner pastors become the recipients of one-sided intimacy. As Diane Marshall notes, they "enter in an ongoing way into some of the most secret, sacred, and fragile dimensions of others' lives."[35] The intimacy that comes from sharing one's personal story fosters a special bond that a congregant feels with the pastor.

If a female congregant forges this bond with her male pastor, she may transfer to him feelings left over from a debilitating past, feelings connected with unresolved difficulties in a present relationship or feelings associated with her future relational hopes. The potential for transference is increased when the congregant is herself emotionally needy. Such emotional emptiness may be especially felt by single and divorced women, or by the woman married to a man who has difficulty expressing his feelings or meeting her emotional needs.

The pastor's personality. The tendency of a congregant to develop feelings for her pastor is augmented by the pastor's own people-orientation. According to a recent article in *Christianity Today,* "Research has shown that a large percentage of people who enter the ministry are of a particular personality type: warm, empathetic, attuned to feelings, concerned about relationships."[36] These characteristics are necessary for effectiveness in ministry, and they invite intimacy from congregants. Most congregations expect that the minister be a sympathetic, understanding, nurturing, caring person. But these traits can also open the door to an unhealthy relationship with a congregant.

Peter Rutter describes the psychological dynamic that may ensue: "A male therapist, pastor or teacher may be the first man in her life who listens to her, encourages her, and teaches her how to develop her own strength. When a woman feels from a man this enlivening quality of recognition for who she really is, her fantasy of hope begins to be fulfilled and she endows their relationship with immeasurable value."[37] If in response the women expresses these newfound feelings, she may proceed to signal an openness to a sexual relationship, or the pastor may interpret her expression of feeling as such an invitation.

Emotional and spiritual burnout. The pastor who is unaware of this dynamic may easily misinterpret the feelings of a female congregant as an indication of romantic or sexual interest. This may especially arise if the demands of caregiving have drained him to the point when he feels that a sexual encounter will yield the emotional and ego satisfaction he needs.[38]

Many pastors are woefully unprepared to handle this situation. Ministers are not always cognizant of the emotional power over the lives of congregants, especially their counselees, that their role generally brings to them. Nor are they always aware when they themselves have reached an emotionally vulnerable situation.

Stan Skarsten describes the dangerous psychological dynamic that so readily occurs as an interplay of transference ("the feelings, tone or attitude of the client towards the counsellor") and countertransference ("the feelings and attitudes that flow from the counsellor toward the client"). He notes that a woman counselee may come to feel that her male counselor "can meet all her unfulfilled needs." However, "if the male therapist accepts this distortion because of his own unresolved sexual needs they are then in for trouble."[39] Skarsten rightly concludes that the male counselor must be aware of his own sexuality and deal with his own needs in order to avoid crossing the line and turning the relationship into a physical one.[40]

Clearly the ministerial role places a pastor in a sexually vulnerable position. A congregant may become attracted to him for a variety of reasons—the intimacy of working together, the transference of feelings to the one who represents God to her, the warmth and care she experiences in his presence, or her desire for an ideal relationship with an ideal man. The pastor, in turn, may sense an attraction to the congregant, triggered by his own emotional needs, the seductiveness of a lonely or single churchgoer, or even the adventure of an illicit sexual liaison.

The pastor who does not understand his vulnerability is either naive or consciously courting a fall. When a pastor finds himself sharing his own problems and personal life with a female congregant, desires to spend more time with her, finds himself fantasizing about her and notes that genuine emotional exchange with his wife has decreased, he should immediately take steps to put the brakes on the developing relationship.

Peter L. Steinke offers this chilling appraisal:

> Without exception, the clergy involved in the sexual affairs asserted that they could have terminated the affairs at any time. But none had ended the alliance until discovered or confronted. All portrayed this sense of omnipotence. They underestimated the power of attachment needs and emotional forces; they overestimated their power to disentangle themselves.[41]

Paul's warning is clear: "So, if you think you are standing firm, be careful that you don't fall!" (1 Corinthians 10:12).

Sexual Addiction and Fantasy

In asking what contributes to clergy sexual misconduct we cannot avoid the possibility that on occasion the offending pastor may be caught in the snare of sexual addiction. Addiction and its attending corollary, sexual fantasy, can be factors that lead a pastor to transgress the boundary of the forbidden zone.

As Patrick Carnes points out, sexual addiction displays certain striking similarities to alcoholism and drug dependency.[42] Whatever the addiction, an addict repeatedly passes through a four-step cycle—preoccupation, ritualization, compulsive sexual behavior and despair—which intensifies with each repetition.[43] As this occurs, the addict's pathological relationship with a mood-altering experience becomes the central focus of his entire life. Addicts therefore "retreat further from the reality of friends, family and work. Their secret lives become more real than their public lives. What people know is a false identity. Only the individual addict knows the shame of living a double life—the real world and the addict's world."[44]

Low sense of worth and retreat into fantasy. Addicts are plagued by low self-esteem which prohibits them from believing that "other people would care for them or meet their needs if everything was known about them, including the addiction."[45] Addicts seek to cover for their conduct through rationalization, delusion and fantasy. And they can always find a convenient scapegoat to blame for their behavior.

Carnes cautions us, however, not to conclude that everyone "who has a regrettable sexual experience is an addict."[46] Many people behave inappropriately at certain transitional stages in their lives. Other people may demonstrate that they are plagued by a sexual problem, but not necessarily an addiction.

The model of addiction helps us understand certain situations of clergy sexual misconduct. The predator we encountered in Peter Donovan and Pastor Steve demonstrates several symptoms associated with sexual addiction. The chemically dependent person provides a helpful parallel to the pastor who lacks the internal mechanism enabling him to see that he is risking everything by entering into a sexual relationship with a congregant. Like the addict, the predator leads a double life, and his actions, rooted as they are in his personality, follow Carnes's "four-step cycle."

In contrast, the wanderer—our Pastor Paul—is not suffering from sexual addiction. In a moment of temptation and weakness he yielded to sexual temptation. Having put this mistake behind him, he is unlikely to repeat the misconduct in the future.

Pornography and fantasies of the forbidden. While not yet repeat offenders, some pastors may find themselves en route to sexual addiction. Pastor Jim's involvement in pornography, for example, may not yet have marked him as an addict, but it ought to have warned him that he faces the potential of future problems. Nor did his one act of adultery seal his fate as a predator. But from that moment on, the danger of addictive behavior began to hang over his life and ministry. Jim needs immediate help.

Related to sexual addiction is the phenomenon of sexual fantasy. Recent studies indicate that fantasy is often a crucial element in sexual failure. Does this mean that sexual fantasy is a sign of addiction and therefore ought to be avoided?

Some Christians strictly warn against fantasy. John White, for example, claims that Jesus' statement—"But I tell you that anyone who looks at a woman lustfully has already committed adultery with her in his heart" (Matthew 5:28)—constitutes a biblical prohibition. But White then clarifies that the focus of our Lord's concern is not thoughts "stirred by the cover of a pornographic magazine" but rather allowing oneself "to play lustfully with the idea of having a relationship with a flesh and blood man or woman whom I know personally."[47]

Other Christians follow the lead of Masters and Johnson, who demonstrate a much more generous view of fantasy.[48] In their estimation, the practice "allows us to escape from the frustrations and limits of our everyday lives. Through fantasy, a person can transform the real world into whatever he or she likes, no matter how briefly or improbably—fantasy can help people find excitement, adventure, self confidence, and pleasure."[49] This positive appraisal finds echo in Tim Stafford. Writing in *Christianity Today,* he claims that fantasy can be healthy, for "surely no one ever consummated a marriage without thinking of it in advance."[50]

Despite their openness to fantasy, Masters and Johnson admit that it plays a major role in deviant sexual behavior, which they term *paraphilia:* "Paraphilia is a condition in which a person's sexual arousal and gratification depend on a fantasy theme of an unusual sexual experience that becomes the principal focus of sexual behavior."[51] When fantasy becomes "necessary for sexual arousal," they argue, the focus is no longer one's partner but one's fantasy.

But more disturbing than the negative effect of fantasy on marital sex is its connection to pornography. Masters and Johnson, as well as Judith Balswick, report this connection: "Men seem plagued by depersonalized fantasies or by domination fantasies in which women are enslaved," themes routinely exploited by pornography.[52] According to Patrick Carnes, when fed by pornography, fantasy becomes a major factor in sexual addiction.[53]

Fantasy is obviously an ambiguous practice. At its best, it is a poor substitute for a healthy sexual relationship. At its worst, it can be destructive to marital sex and may open the door to unwholesome behavior, even sexual addiction. It is clearly not merely an innocent pastime, but a symptom of the kind of sexual obsession that creates ruin in many lives.

The ambiguity of fantasy should cause pastors to be cautious about their own involvement in this activity. Unfortunately this is not always the case. *Christianity Today* reports that ministers apparently are more prone than their congregants to fantasize frequently about having sex with someone other than their spouse.[54]

Paul, however, enjoins Christians to "take captive every thought to make it obedient to Christ." (2 Corinthians 10:5) and to focus on "whatever is true, whatever is noble, whatever is right, whatever is pure" (Philippians 4:8). No pastor can provide room and board for a sexual fantasy without eventually discovering that his fantasy life has undermined biblical convictions and values first in his imagination and eventually in his behavior. Unbiblical fantasy opens the door to self-indulgence, robs the pastor of healthy sexual enjoyment, and can begin the process that leads him into sexual misconduct with all its attendant disasters.

Spiritual Dryness

Our exploration of the factors in clergy sexual misconduct remains incomplete until we touch on the spiritual dynamic involved. A pastor is most vulnerable to sexual failure when his spiritual condition has deteriorated. He may have entered a period of spiritual coldness. He may have lost his zeal for personal integrity as a disciple and Christian leader. Or he may have fallen into the trap of believing that he is somehow exempt from the righteous living God expects from every believer. Whatever the situation, his willingness to contemplate inappropriate sexual activity indicates that the pastor has lost his "first love" (Revelation 2:4). He has simply turned away from the Lord as the ultimate source of true fulfillment.

The factors we have enumerated can never fully explain why a particular person falls into sexual misconduct. Nevertheless, these considerations provide a point of departure. Cognizant of the unacknowledged forces that may be at work in his life or the life of a congregant, the concerned pastor can take stock of his own vulnerable situation and take appropriate action to deal positively with the problems he and the congregant face.

Counteracting the Epidemic

Clergy sexual misconduct is the final outcome of a long path traveled by the offending pastor. The path may pass by several observable mileposts:

1. dysfunctional family of origin
2. unreasonable expectations of marriage and spouse
3. acute marital disappointment
4. blaming others, including his wife
5. attraction to pornography and fantasy as a refuge and substitute
6. formation of counseling relationships without safeguards
7. attraction to a sexual liaison as an opportunity to gain intimacy and admiration
8. seizing of the perceived opportunity
9. experiencing the unanticipated consequences of the act of sexual misconduct

More than spiritual giftedness, ministry skills and demonstrated effectiveness, character is the mark of the true messenger of God. The quality of the person, including moral integrity—not merely technical competence—qualifies a person for the ordained office. Paul cautions Timothy that the pastor must be one who not merely "fights the good fight" but engages in ministry "holding on to faith and a good conscience." In this manner the godly pastor can avoid the plight of those who "have shipwrecked their faith" (1 Timothy 1:18-19).

Christian integrity has to do with the integration of sound biblical convictions with outward actions. Moral integrity, of course, is God's ideal for every believer. Yet it is especially imperative for pastors. Being a minister is not a *job* that occupies only a set number of hours per week. It is a *calling* that encompasses all that a person is and does. The pastorate is the one profession that can tolerate no dichotomy between private lifestyle and public conduct. A pastor's personal integrity is—for better or worse—intertwined with professional competence. Nor can a pastor neatly separate his professional conduct from his personal life as a Christian.

Integrity in the pastor's relationship to congregants means above all trustworthiness. Congregants desire and need pastors who are honest, fair and helpful. They want to believe that their pastor always seeks their good, even at the expense of his personal gain. They want a pastor whom they can trust never to act to hurt anyone in the flock.

Clergy sexual misconduct breaks this trust. It is a violation of the integrity of the pastorate. The betrayal of trust occurs in two related dimensions of interpersonal life—sexuality and power. It involves simultaneously a violation of sexuality and an abuse of power.

In the following pages we turn our attention first to developing a theological understanding of the problem by viewing its sexual and power components (chapters three and four). Then in the remaining three chapters we focus on practical response, seeking ways in which we can minister to the victims, assist pastors in prevention and finally advise churches on how best to deal with misconduct.

3
Misconduct as Betrayal of a Sexual Trust

exual misconduct assumes many forms. It may begin with sexualized behavior or *sexual approach*—verbal or nonverbal acts or statements conveying sexual interest or intending to express or arouse erotic interest. Sometimes sexual approach leads to *sexual harassment*. Harassment includes any act through which the perpetrator uses his (or her) power over the victim to manipulate or control the situation or to present a threat to the personal or professional well-being of the victim.[1] Sexual misconduct is especially devastating when it entails *sexual contact*, that is, overt physical acts which arouse or satisfy sexual desire.

When a male pastor exploits the inherent privilege of his position for personal sexual ends, his activity—whether seemingly innocent sexual approach, obnoxious harassment or actual contact—is abusive. He has strayed beyond the bounds of acceptable conduct.

On occasion the offending minister may fail to see that his actions constitute misconduct, claiming instead that sexual activity in this specific situation is warranted. More often, however, clergy sexual abuse results from a failure of integrity. It occurs because the minister has silenced the voice of Christian conviction in order to act in violation of ethical standards that he himself otherwise acknowledges.

Regardless of how it happens, clergy sexual misconduct entails a violation of the integrity of the pastorate, and hence a betrayal of the ordination vow. It marks a breaking of the trust that normally exists between pastor and people. The betrayal of trust involves both an abuse of sexuality and an abuse of power.

In this chapter we look at the phenomenon of clergy misconduct as an abuse of human sexuality, a violation of ourselves as sexual beings. Viewed from this perspective it entails a betrayal of sexual trust.

At the heart of misconduct is a failure in understanding and applying the foundational Christian teaching about human sexuality. To understand this problem, therefore, we must place clergy sexual misconduct within the context of a biblical view of ourselves as sexual creatures.

Cultural Patterns of Sexuality

Theorists are becoming increasingly aware that socialization patterns are partly to blame for the epidemic of sexual misconduct in our society. Such patterns are important because our sexuality is not merely a given; it is also a construct that comes with the development of personhood. Our sense of sexual identity is the culmination of an interaction between our internal physical or biological makeup and external social or cultural influences.[2]

Traditionally our culture has entrusted females with the task of setting sexual boundaries while encouraging males to push against these same boundaries. For this reason, sexual activity almost inherently carries elements of conquest and refusal, and hence a power dimension. Further, we are socialized to believe that in any sexual relation one person (the male) must be dominant and the other (the female) subordinate. This erroneous idea promotes coercion and manipulation, and it inculturates both men and women to link sexual activity and violence. As Pamela Cooper-White notes, "All young men are socialized to some degree to see women as prey, seductresses who will say No and mean Yes."[3] Violence, in turn, becomes eroticized, as violent and abusive acts (especially against women) themselves trigger sexual arousal in men.[4]

As a result of these cultural dynamics, any relationship in which a male and a female enter with an inequality of power is potentially an arena for abuse. Because in our society males generally hold greater power in such relationships and because the male is the one socialized to exercise power in sexual exploits, males tend to be the main perpetrators. Rather than being inherently immune by virtue of ordination and the clergy office, male pastors are vulnerable to the temptation to cross the boundary that separates wholesome relations with female congregants from inappropriate or even abusive liaisons with them.

The minister who would maintain trust and integrity must be keenly aware of his own sexuality and continually monitor his sexual needs.[5] But the problem of sexual misconduct among clergy—like the wider phenomenon of sexual abuse in society—lies deeper. At its root are the socialization patterns present in our culture. Thus, as Theis notes, beyond treatment, early detection and intervention, the long-term solution includes "deconstructing a flawed template and reconstructing new possibilities."[6] The problem of clergy sexual misconduct demands that the church lead the way "into an ongoing process of discovering the pitfalls of the current construction of male sexuality in the broader culture generally and within the subculture of the church specifically."[7]

We believe that the foundation for the radical reorientation practitioners are advocating includes a renewed appreciation for the biblical understanding of sexuality.[8]

The Nature of Human Sexuality

Human beings are sexual creatures. Contrary to the view of many persons in our society, our sexuality lies deeper than the physical characteristics and activities associated with male and female reproductive roles. Sexuality encompasses our fundamental existence in the world as embodied persons, including our way of being in and relating to the world as male or female. Sexuality also lies at the foundation of our sensuality—our ability to appreciate the world around us.

Above all, however, sexuality is connected to our incompleteness as embodied creatures, which biological sex symbolizes. This connection means that sexuality lies behind the human quest for completeness, expressed through the drive toward bonding. Of course, the dynamic of sexuality brings male and female together in the unity of persons we know as marriage. But the yearning for completeness also forms the basis of the interpersonal dimension of existence.

The biblical documents reflect this understanding of the dynamic of sexuality. According to the second Genesis narrative, the creation of the woman was God's solution to Adam's predicament. Although the man enjoyed a relationship with the animals, none was an appropriate bonding partner for him. God desired to create another who could deliver Adam from his isolation. In contrast to his response to the animals, the male immediately sensed a bond with the female, which led him to burst forth in the joyous declaration: She is "bone of my bones and flesh of my flesh." The narrator concludes the episode with an application to the phenomenon of male-female bonding: "For this reason a man will leave his father and mother and be united to his wife, and they will become one flesh" (v. 24). This intimate bond of husband and wife, in turn, marked a first step toward the establishment of the broader human community, including the tribe and eventually the nation.

In the New Testament era, Jesus inaugurated a change in outlook. He left his physical family for the sake of his mission in the kingdom of God, counting as his true family "whoever does the will of my Father in heaven" (Matthew 12:50). In keeping with his own example, the Nazarene challenged his followers to place their relationship to him above all familial ties (Matthew 10:37). At the same time, he promised to the loyal disciple a spiritual community to compensate for the loss entailed in leaving family for the sake of discipleship (Mark 10:29-30). Jesus' teaching means that in God's design the primary human bond is no longer the physical family but the company of disciples. More important than physical ancestry (who one's parents are) is one's spiritual ancestry (who one's heavenly Father is). In every era Jesus challenges his disciples to direct their highest loyalty to him so that their primary relationship is the bond uniting them to him and to the community of his followers.

The Bible leads us to conclude that whatever expression it may take, our sexuality is the primary force that brings us out of our isolation into relationship with others. This drive toward bonding leads to the development of social communities, beginning with marriage and family, but including other bonding relationships as well. Our quest for completeness finds ultimate fulfillment, however, only through participation in the community of believers who enjoy fellowship with God through Christ. Consequently, our sense of incompleteness—our sexuality—forms the dynamic lying behind the search for truth. This quest ultimately becomes the search for the God who created us to find completion in fellowship with each other and with our Maker and Savior. As Augustine noted so profoundly, "Our hearts are restless until they find rest in thee, O God."

Our human restlessness, related as it is to our fundamental sexuality, points forward to the consummation of God's activity in the community of his eternal kingdom. In the meantime he has ordained two alternative contexts for the expression of our sexuality—marriage and singleness.

Sexuality and Marriage

Marriage is not a specifically Christian institution, for it is present in some form in all human societies. In fact, the opening chapters of the book of Genesis indicate that marriage has been a part of human existence from the beginning.

Some people view marriage primarily as the context for sexual expression. This understanding can claim a scriptural foundation. According to the Bible marriage is the proper context for the sex act and forms the boundary within which God intends that the sex drive be exercised. The Old Testament law codified this view, and Jesus and the New Testament writers reaffirmed it. Other people connect marriage with procreation and child-rearing. This view has been especially influential within the Roman Catholic Church, which teaches that openness to procreation forms the only context in which sexual intercourse is legitimate.

Perhaps the most widely held understanding in contemporary society sees marriage as the focus of companionship. In the ideal marriage, proponents declare, husband and wife grow to be closest friends; they experience intimacy, enjoy being together and share interests, goals and dreams. Christian advocates can appeal to the second creation narrative (Genesis 2) and the stories of the Hebrew patriarchs, such as Abraham and Sarah, Isaac and Rebekah, Jacob and Rachel, as well as Ruth and Boaz. While companionship may be crucial to the marital bond, the focus on this dimension is not without dangers. It exposes marriage to the self-centered, individualistic and self-actualizing tendencies characteristic of our society.

Although these suggestions reflect valid dimensions of the purposes of marriage, none of them captures the central role that this relationship fulfills in God's purposes. The Creator's goal in instituting marriage ultimately lies in God's desire to enter into covenantal fellowship with human beings who thereby enjoy community with each other and with their Savior. Marriage advances this divine program for humankind.

Beginning with the Fall and climaxing with Jesus' birth in Bethlehem, marriage advanced the divine program by serving as the means for bringing into the world God's Son, the hope of a redeemed humanity. While driving them out of the Garden of Eden, God gave our first parents a promise: the Redeemer would be the child of the woman. From Eve to Mary, God's promise was kept alive through the procreation of generation after generation of his covenant people. "When the time had fully come," the home established by Joseph and Mary cradled the birth and childhood of the virgin-conceived Redeemer.

Since the coming of Christ, marriage has functioned in the program of God in a second manner. It is now a vehicle for the development and expansion of the divine community as focused in Christ's church, and it is an expression of the expansive nature and outreach mandate of the church. Marriage serves as an agent for the expansion of the church through the influence of the Christian in the home, both as a believing spouse (1 Corinthians 7:12-16; 1 Peter 3:1-6) and as a godly parent (Ephesians 6:4). The New Testament also speaks of marriage as a vehicle for the outreach mission of the church, as Christian families exercise a positive influence in the wider society. (New Testament examples include Lydia [Acts 16:11-15, 25-34, 40], Philemon, and Priscilla and Aquila [Acts 18:2-3, 26; Romans 16:3; 1 Corinthians 16:19].)

Above all, however, the Bible presents marriage as a metaphor of spiritual truth. The biblical writers appeal to the husband-wife bond to symbolize certain aspects of the relation between God and God's people. The Old Testament prophets found marriage an appropriate vehicle for telling the story of Yahweh and Israel. The narrative opens with the betrothal of Israel to Yahweh. God intended that Israel be like a virgin bride who gives herself willingly, continually and exclusively to her husband (Jeremiah 2:2) and thereby becomes his delight (Isaiah 62:5). But Israel showed herself to be an unfaithful, adulterous spouse, forsaking Yahweh for other gods (Jeremiah 3:6, 8; Hosea 2:2, 4-5). Despite Israel's "adultery," Yahweh remained faithful, even promising a future restoration or renewal of the relationship (Hosea 2:23).

The New Testament authors drew from this Old Testament imagery (for example, Romans 9:25; 1 Peter 2:9-10) and poured additional theological significance into the marital bond. For them marriage forms a picture of the great mystery of salvation—the union of Christ and the church. The ideal marriage illustrates the mystery of Christ's self-sacrifice for the church and the church's submission to Christ (Ephesians 5:21-33).

Related to marriage as an illustration of the mystery of Christ's relationship to the church is the imagery of the bridegroom and the bride (John 3:29; Mark 2:18-20), whose marriage will be consummated in the future (Revelation 19:7; 21:9-10; 21:2). Hence, the fellowship that God intended from the beginning, to which marriage has always borne witness, is ultimately fulfilled in the new society at the end of salvation history. Marriage is a symbol of that future reality. As male and female maintain the marital bond in all fidelity, they provide a picture of the grand future fellowship of the redeemed humanity with the Creator. A good marriage is a foretaste and sign on a small scale of the great community God is bringing to pass. So even in the present, marriage is to be a foreshadowing or precursory experience of the community God intends to create.

Viewed from the New Testament perspective, marriage also declares the holy nature of God's love. As a spiritual metaphor, the marital union forms a picture of the bond of love that is present within the triune God and that overflows from God to creation. More specifically, the exclusive love shared by husband and wife reflects the holiness of the divine love. Marital love is a picture of the exclusive love present within the Trinity. Marriage is likewise an appropriate picture of the exclusive relationship God desires to share with his people. The marital bond is special and must be held inviolate. In the same way, the believer's relationship to God must be holy. As God's covenant people, we can have no other gods but the one God (Exodus 20:3), for this God alone is worthy of our love, worship and service.

God instituted marriage as the context for sexual expression, for the procreation and nurturing of children and for lifelong companionship between man and woman. But above all, God intends that the marital bond serve the divine purpose in bringing about community. As husbands and wives live together in the marital relationship, their life together can be a picture of the mystery of Christ and the church, as well as of the reality of the divine love. Therefore, we must hold marriage in high regard, because God intends that it be a grand symbol and foretaste of the central truth of our faith. No wonder Jesus asserted that the Creator's ideal is the monogamous, faithful union of a male and a female in a lifelong commitment to one another.

Sexuality and Singleness

The lofty Christian understanding of sexuality also provides insight into the other human life context, singleness. Like marriage, singleness has a place in the divine program. In fact, marriage and singleness are two valid contexts for expressing our identity as sexual beings.

Singleness does not refer to a uniform experience, however. The term can refer to the beginning stage of each human life, the years before a person is eligible for marriage. Primarily, singleness depicts the ongoing unmarried existence in adulthood, even if that state is not due to a person's conscious choice. At the same time, singleness also may denote the existence resulting from a personal decision. This includes the choice of celibacy as a means to some higher end, such as service to the church in clergy or missionary roles or as a means to speak against some aspect of modern Western society. Finally, the term includes the unmarried state that follows when a person's marriage has ended, whether through divorce or the death of one's spouse.

The ancient Hebrew society clearly viewed marriage as the norm and gave little place to single persons. However, the New Testament elevated singleness, presenting the single life as one means through which believers can fulfill their divine vocation. John the Baptist, Paul and above all Jesus carried out their God-given missions within the divine economy as single persons. They provide rich indication that singleness is no barrier to service in God's program.

In discussing marriage, Paul took the matter a step farther. Based on pragmatic considerations, he advised that the single life may in certain circumstances be preferable to marriage. Singleness offers flexibility to do the Lord's work (1 Corinthians 7:32-35), given "the present crisis" (v. 26). Even the widow, he added, "is happier if she stays as she is" (v. 40).

The role of singleness in the economy of God, however, is larger than pragmatic considerations. Like marriage, this life context also carries theological meaning.

To understand the significance of singleness, we must keep in mind that as embodied persons all humans are sexual creatures, whether or not they engage in sex. Because the deeper reality of our sexuality remains operative, single persons who are not sexually active remain sexual beings (even though our society finds it difficult to view priests and "old maids" as sexual creatures). Single people continue to see themselves as male or female, and this affects their way of relating to the world, to other persons and to themselves.

More significantly, single persons also experience bonding—the deeper level of human sexuality that we seek because of our fundamental incompleteness, our inner restlessness and our desire for love and intimacy. Single persons experience bonding on different levels and in several ways, including the bonding of friendship and, for the believer, the bonding within the community of Christ. The bonding indicative of the single life, however, differs from the marital relationship. Single bonding is neither permanent nor exclusive, it is seldom entered through formal covenant, and it is not to be expressed in genital sexual activity.

The single person's drive to bond provides the foundation for the significance of singleness within God's program. The single life provides powerful imagery of the universal, nonexclusive and expanding nature of God's love. In contrast to the marital union, single persons form bonds that are less defined and therefore more open to the inclusion of others. Further, the "family" formed by the love of single persons is not the product of the intimate sexual acts shared by two people but the spontaneous dynamic of a love that is open beyond exclusive boundaries. The less formal bonding of single persons reflects the openness of God's love that seeks to include within the circle of fellowship those yet outside its boundaries. Hence, the single life can express the nonexclusive aspect of the divine love.

Singleness, like marriage, also expresses God's goal of establishing community, but again in a different manner. The fellowship God desires to share with human beings is exclusive. The Bible speaks of a "jealous God," one who demands holiness and hates idolatry. The community God's activity brings into existence, therefore, is a fellowship characterized by an intimate bond between God and humans. Marriage represents God's intent to form a community of fellowship on the basis of exclusive love and fidelity.

At the same time, rather than being limited to a few, God's community is open to "whosoever will." As long as it remains incomplete, God cannot rest. The loving God is always seeking the outsider so that still more persons can enjoy the divine fellowship. Singleness portrays this dynamic. The single life represents the expansive nature of the purposes of God, who seeks to bring each person into the community God is establishing.

Sexuality and the Sex Act

Many people have a truncated view of sexuality. Sex, they believe, is merely an activity, something we do that does not affect who we are. They see the sex act primarily as a means to self-actualization and self-expression.[9]

Contemporary thinkers, however, are growing uneasy with the modern reduction of sexuality to an activity. An increasing number of psychologists now maintain that sex without "commitment" is dehumanizing.[10] More importantly, many are convinced that the sex act is a highly meaningful metaphor. It symbolizes our union with or our possession of the other, which union holds out the promise of completing what we lack as finite, incomplete selves.

The understanding of the sex act as metaphor comes from a contemporary theory as to what meaning is and how meaning develops. This view maintains that events are meaningful only as they are imbedded within a larger context. By extension, the meaning of a human act is dependent on the context in which it transpires, which is closely related to the intent of the actor.[11]

This theory has important ramifications for understanding the sex act. The meaning of sexual intercourse is dependent on its context. The participants pour meaning into the act by the intent that motivates them and by the context they create when they engage in it.

The inherent relationship between act and context means that the sex act cannot be separated from the personhood of the human beings who engage in it. Sex is not something that happens at a distance from the person. Like human actions in general, sexual intercourse is an expression of the intent of the actor who creates a context for the action, from which, in turn, the act derives its meaning.

Biblical Sexuality and Sexual Misconduct

Christians take this dynamic a step farther. We realize that we do not simply *create* the context in which our actions take on meaning. Rather, we view ourselves as creatures before God and participants in the community of Christ. We are deeply aware that what we do is important, for our actions are expressions of our being. For this reason, the Christian takes the Pauline admonition seriously: "Do you not know that your body is a temple of the Holy Spirit, who is in you, whom you have received from God? You are not your own; you were bought at a price. Therefore honor God with your body" (1 Corinthians 6:19-20).

Thus we must understand our involvement in sex within the context of the Christian life as a whole. We must place sexual expression within the parameters of our fundamental commitment to the lordship of Christ. Viewed in this manner, the sex act becomes a powerful theological statement. It speaks about the self, about the nature of life and ultimately about God.

The Christian ethic maintains that God has set parameters for sex, which in turn contribute to its intended meaning. The true meaning of sexual intercourse discloses itself within a proper context (marriage) and with a proper intent (to express unconditional, covenantal love). Practiced within this context, sexual intercourse can be a beautiful symbol of mutual commitment and mutual submission, as through this act husband and wife reaffirm their commitment to each other. Further, the sex act within marriage can become a beautiful celebration of the marital relationship enjoyed by the marriage partners. And it can express their openness to the new life that may arise from their bond.

When practiced apart from the context of a loving marriage, the sex act also carries meaning. But the meanings it derives from the nonmarital context are quite different from what God intends. Rather than being the beautiful symbol of covenantal love God designed it to be, sex outside of marriage all too readily becomes an expression of self-gratification, infidelity or exploitation.

A Christian Sex Ethic for Our Day

According to the biblical ideal, the proper context for genital sexual expression is the bond of a loving marriage. As a result, the traditional Christian sex ethic advocates abstinence in singleness and fidelity in marriage. But in what sense does the Christian ethic assist us in coming to terms with the contemporary problem of clergy sexual misconduct?

Recent decades have been marked by widespread rejection of biblical teachings and norms. In the face of the new reality, many Christian thinkers advocate that we simply discard the traditional Christian sex ethic as no longer workable.[12] They replace the older emphasis on abstinence in singleness and fidelity in marriage with what they see as more applicable norms.

Marie Fortune offers a typical example. A strong advocate of mutual consent, she writes, "The only *rule* that should guide one's sexual decision-making and behavior is 'thou shalt not sexually manipulate, abuse, or take advantage of another at any time.' "[13] Fortune correctly warns that any relationship—including marriage—can be exploitive and therefore that even marital partners must acknowledge the principle of mutual consent. Contemporary statements, such as Fortune's, offer a welcome corrective to the misapplication of the traditional ethic. Yet by discarding the older emphasis on abstinence and fidelity, they do not provide a sufficient response to the problem of clergy sexual misconduct.

Contemporary reformulations are generally insufficient in that they condone impermanent sexual relations, which are always potentially exploitive. In attempting to counter the abuses critics claim are spawned by the traditional ethic, the newer views open the door for other abuses. Rather than fostering nonmanipulative relationships, the implicit or explicit approval of sexual activity beyond the boundaries of marriage, which contemporary statements embody, compounds the difficulty of building healthy male-female sexual bonds. Fortune herself admits that "freely chosen, fully informed, and mutually agreed upon sexual activity with another might in fact be a rare experience."[14]

We maintain that the traditional Christian ethic places men and women in the best position to grow into the kind of mutual relationships Fortune and others advocate. This ethical standard increases—rather than decreases—the likelihood of creating relationships characterized by mutual consent. The unconditional commitment of husband and wife is more likely to provide a nurturing context in which trust and mutuality are free to grow than even the most intimate male-female relationship apart from marriage.

In addition to introducing new potentials for sexual manipulation, contemporary reformulations tend to be deficient. Focusing on the negative, they fail to grasp the positive intention of the traditional ethic. God's concern does not end with the prevention of manipulation and abuse in sexual relations. Rather, the Creator desires that the sex act carry certain positive meanings associated with a permanent, loving sexual bond. Our God desires that sexual intercourse be a celebration of an inviolate, loving relationship between a man and a woman who are unconditionally committed to each other, for this bond symbolizes God's loving covenant with us.

Sexual misconduct has become widespread among clergy partially because the church has let go of the biblical understanding of human sexuality and consequently has lost its ethical moorings. By failing to show how abstinence and fidelity are based in the good purposes of the Creator for humankind, traditional Christian moralists have made the biblical standards appear arbitrary. By discarding the traditional standards under the pressure of the secular world and the widespread rejection of biblical norms, modern Christian thinkers have contributed to the confusion. Without a clear articulation of biblical standards of sexual behavior as arising from God's design for human welfare, ministers possess neither a solid foundation for pastoral care nor a sense of clear and appropriate boundaries for their own conduct.

Don S. Browning offers this penetrating analysis: "The major difficulty with the pastoral care of the church today is that ministers are attempting to care for and counsel persons without the support of a fund of meanings that provide the context of understanding for the problems that the minister and the congregation are facing."[15] He notes that this is especially acute in sexual matters:

> Our visions about what marriage should be are so vague that the counselor . . . often feels unable to assume anything normative. He must content

himself with the more technical emotional-dynamic dimensions which do not interfere with the increasingly more pluralistic value commitments of people in our society on this issue. It should be the virtue of the church, and of the care and counseling which proceed under its auspices, that it would provide this context of normative meaning so increasingly difficult to achieve in our pluralistic and rapidly changing society. But the same forces that make it increasingly difficult for the secular counselor to assume a framework of normative meanings also strongly affect the capacity of the church to create and maintain a fund of normative meanings even for its members, not to mention the larger society.[16]

Despite its widespread rejection today, the traditional Christian ethic grounded on a positive understanding of humans as sexual beings has not lost its importance as the foundation for sexual relations. Viewed in the light of this ethic, sexual misconduct on the part of pastors is a violation of God's design for human sexual expression. It is the betrayal of a sexual trust. The road to wholeness and healing begins with an unconditional commitment to abstinence by single pastors and to marital fidelity on the part of married clergy. Such commitment, however, cannot be simply arbitrary. It must be grounded on a personal awareness of how abstinence and fidelity fulfill God's design for the pastor's life and ministry as a sexual creature.

Fidelity and the Married Pastor

Sexual misconduct among clergy is a betrayal of sexual trust. The first step in finding a way through the problem lies in pastors' understanding themselves as sexual beings and committing themselves to following biblical standards. For the married pastor this necessitates an uncompromising personal commitment to marital fidelity.

Commitment to marital fidelity is crucial because it provides the standard against which a pastor can appraise any act he might consider engaging in with a female congregant. Measured against the standard of fidelity, sexual indiscretion always is a violation of trust.

For a married pastor the most blatant act of indiscretion, of course, is adultery. Some people have attempted to put a positive face on certain occurrences of extramarital sexual intercourse. But when viewed against the standard of fidelity, any involvement in the sex act beyond the boundaries of marriage violates the marital bond.

The violative nature of adultery emerges from our earlier discussion of the contextual meaning of sexual intercourse. We noted that the context of an act, including a sexual act, contributes to its meaning. Within the context of a loving marital relationship, sexual intercourse can convey a divinely intended meaning. Outside of marriage, however, the act is no longer able to symbolize or be the reaffirmation of the marital vow, for no such covenant unites the adulterous pair. It cannot be the joyful celebration of the unconditional commitment of man and woman because the partners have made no such explicit commitment to each other. On the contrary, a commitment was made by at least one of the two persons to another.

The meaning of infidelity. Although an adulterous relationship cannot state what the sex act is intended to declare, it is not for that reason devoid of meaning. When it occurs in the context of an extramarital relationship, the sex act is a vivid proclamation of the violation of the marriage bond, voiced by both participants. This act embodies the married pastor's disregard for the commitment he once made to his spouse, as well as his partner's contempt of that marriage bond. Through this act, both participants violate the personhood of the pastor's wife.

In the context of an extramarital relationship, the sex act also symbolizes the fallenness of the marriage. Adultery declares that the relationship has failed to reflect God's ideal. It embodies the adulterous spouse's hopeless abandonment of his marriage, as well as his conclusion that because he cannot find complete sexual fellowship with his marriage partner he must seek fulfillment from another. Because of the grave consequences of adultery for the marital bond, through this act the unfaithful spouse may also be voicing his unwillingness to work at restoring the fallen marriage.

Finally, within the context of an extramarital relationship the sex act symbolizes the adulterous pastor's fallen relationship to his spouse. In the context of marriage the sex act symbolizes the desire of husband and wife to give and receive fulfillment. In the context of adultery the act symbolizes the desire of one spouse to seek personal sexual fulfillment without fulfilling the needs of his spouse. Viewed from the context of the marriage, adulterous sex marks the triumph of eros over agape, as he places his desire for the other woman above his pledge to accept his wife unconditionally and to fulfill her needs.

The significance of fidelity. In addition to the grave meanings it embodies, adulterous sex also carries theological overtones. To understand this we must compare the theological significance of fidelity and unfaithfulness, for a person's sexual conduct brings to light his (or her) fundamental theological beliefs or outlooks toward the nature of reality.

For example, sexual conduct reveals a person's fundamental belief about the nature of humankind. The one who engages in extramarital sexual relationships sets out on the path to sexual solitude. By engaging in sex apart from long-term commitment, a person risks reducing his sexual partners to objects that move in and out of his life. Casual sex reduces other persons to the status of objects that the ego-self uses to fulfill perceived needs. In this manner, involvement in adultery asserts that the solitary ego constitutes the final human reality.

Sexual fidelity, in contrast, affirms that the corporate dimension, rather than the solitary ego, is central to human existence. Fidelity embodies a person's realization of the importance of reciprocal relations among humans and the coincidence of give-and-take. It asserts that fulfilling the other while being fulfilled by the other lies at the heart of human existence. To be human, fidelity declares, means fundamentally to live in relationship with others.

Sexual conduct likewise reveals a person's understanding of the nature of ultimate reality. To engage in adulterous sex is to imply that the universe (or whatever powers are thought to be at work in the world) is fundamentally capricious. Despite the apparent order in the world, it is ultimately disorderly, and whatever lies behind the universe (if anything or anyone) is unfaithful and untrustworthy. Adultery declares that God cannot be trusted. The Creator either does not enter into covenant with humankind or cannot be trusted to be faithful to this covenant.

Sexual fidelity, in contrast, affirms the eternal faithfulness of God. By being faithful to each other, a married couple indicate that they believe that the divine covenant partner is faithful to the people of the covenant. For this reason the covenant between male and female in the fellowship of marriage forms a fitting analogy of the relationship between Christ and the church (Ephesians 5:22-33).

The biblical use of marriage as a picture of the divine-human relation leads us to understand the grave theological pain that adultery inflicts. Marital unfaithfulness is a grievous act not merely because it is a violation of human personhood but also because it defaces a divinely ordained symbol representing the relation God wants to enjoy with humans. Because God intends that the covenant between husband and wife assist us in understanding the mutuality Christ seeks to enjoy with his disciples, marital unfaithfulness is a serious matter. It undermines the theological purpose that God intended for this human relationship.

Any person guilty of adultery has broken a sexual trust. He has violated his spouse, his partner and himself as sexual beings. And he has effaced the grand theological picture God intends marriage to provide. But a pastor who engages in sexual misconduct has also betrayed a sexual trust bound up with his position as an ordained church leader. Because of the role of clergy as "examples to the flock," ministers are to model to the community what it means to live in sexual fidelity. The adulterous pastor, however, has violated this holy calling.

Abstinence and the Single Pastor

For the married pastor, concern to live out the biblical understanding of sexuality necessitates an uncompromising commitment to marital fidelity. For the single pastor, sexual loyalty begins with an equally uncompromising commitment to abstinence, born from an understanding of himself as a sexual being. The call for abstinence is unpopular, even contemptible, in contemporary society and increasingly so in the church as well. Nevertheless, abstinence remains the foundation for the avoidance of the breach of sexual trust involved in misconduct perpetrated by single clergy.

The necessity of abstinence. Several considerations point out the importance of abstinence for the unmarried pastor. Abstinence is crucial because of its close relationship to the advantages of singleness for ministry. Paul declares that the single life facilitates wholehearted involvement in the program of God in the world (1 Corinthians 7:32-35). Because the single pastor is not sidetracked by concern for a spouse, he is able to devote full attention to the affairs of the Lord.

The single pastor who does not practice abstinence, however, loses this advantage. Although he remains legally unmarried, the presence of a sexual partner in his life reintroduces the element of concern for the interests of another that Paul found among married persons. In fact, the concerns triggered by the presence of a sexual partner in the life of a single person can actually surpass what is present in marriage. In contrast to the stability of relationship that marriage ideally introduces, the relationship between a single person and his "significant other" is inherently unstable. The impermanency of this situation leads to anxieties about personal performance or worries about the future of the relationship, as well as a sense of competition with sexual rivals, all of which the permanent nature of marital commitment ideally eliminates.

More important than this pragmatic consideration, abstinence is crucial to the single pastor because singleness is not a proper context for the sex act. According to the understanding of human sexuality presented in this chapter, sexual intercourse must be limited to the loving relationship between husband and wife. Only in that context can the act can carry its divinely intended meanings.

This is not to say that apart from marriage the sex act is devoid of meaning. Were this so, we might possibly agree with those who argue that unmarried persons could engage in the act merely for the sake of pleasure. To assert that the sex act is purely recreational is to deny our embodied existence; it is to suggest that sexual intercourse is an act of the body that does not involve our inner selves. But as we noted earlier, the sex act is not merely a function of the body. It is an act of our whole selves as sexual beings and therefore always carries some meaning.

When it occurs outside the boundary of a loving relationship between two married persons, the positive meanings God designed the sex act to carry are replaced by other connotations. These are at best poor substitutes for its ideal meaning, and often they constitute an outright denial of the intended meaning of the act.

For example, outside a loving marriage relationship sexual intercourse expresses the concept of bonding without permanency; it represents an impermanent and nonbinding covenant, which is simply a contradiction. Further, when an unmarried person engages in sex he makes a false declaration about the depth of the relationship he shares with his partner. As a symbol of the permanent marital bond, sexual intercourse is a "life-uniting act" that seals the relationship between male and female. Sex outside of marriage, however, involves two people in a life-uniting act who do not have a life-uniting intent.[17] Hence, through this act they proclaim that a life-uniting commitment is present where no such intent exists.

Above all, abstinence is crucial for the unmarried pastor because of the theological metaphor God intends singleness to be. We have argued that the single life can serve as a picture of God's expansive love and the divine concern to establish an inclusive community. Abstinence is crucial to the metaphorical significance of singleness, for it is an appropriate reminder of the nonexclusive nature of the divine love. By abstaining from the act that celebrates exclusive bonding while remaining open to forming the bond of friendship with many people, the single person provides a picture of the God whose goal is the establishment of a human community, which although intimate is nevertheless expansive.

Engaging in the sex act within the context of the single life, on the other hand, sets forth an ambiguous assertion about the divine reality. It inserts a sense of nonexclusivity into an act—sexual intercourse—that represents exclusiveness. It also introduces a noninclusive dimension into a life-context—singleness—that should be open to others. As a result, sexual activity within singleness mars the picture of the divine reality that the sex act and the single life are each intended to reflect.

The role of the single pastor as example to others adds an additional urgency to the commitment to abstinence. Just as his married colleague is to model sexual fidelity, so also the unmarried minister is to model to the community sexual integrity as a single person. Sexual misconduct by a single clergyman constitutes a betrayal of the great sexual trust that he accepted at his ordination or when he was called into church leadership.

The possibility of abstinence. Abstinence may be the ideal for the single pastor. But is it attainable? Perhaps in the contemporary climate of sexual fixation, the unmarried minister faces a greater potential for failure than does his married colleague. Marriage offers a married pastor the potential for enjoyment of personal and physical intimacy with a life-partner; this is denied to the single minister. Nevertheless, we are convinced that for no one—married or single—is the biblical ideal unattainable. However, the task of living out the implications of our understanding of sexuality may require greater vigilance in the day-to-day life of a single pastor.

The single pastor who would live with sexual integrity must come to terms with the issue of intimacy in his life. In this process, Protestant pastors can learn from their Roman Catholic counterparts. In his study of priests who enjoy intimacy in the midst of obedience to the vow of celibacy, Tim O'Connell discovered a variety of paths. Some priests find intimacy through group life, including prayer groups, support groups or deeply caring friendship groups. Others meet their intimacy needs through individual relationships. Concerning this, O'Connell notes, "The ways that these relationships define themselves, the specification of the partner (male/female, religious/lay, single/married) and the frequency of interaction, vary widely. But the common denominators are that it is a genuinely reciprocal, self-revelatory relationship, not a disguised occasion for ministry, and that it is a close relationship which does, in fact, meet the intimacy needs of the priest."[18] In a related study

Richard Sipe noted the presence of several elements among Catholic priests who have achieved a truly celibate life: work, prayer, community, service, attention to physical needs, balance, security, order, learning and appreciation of beauty.[19]

In our study of the effects of clergy sexual misconduct in chapter two, we noted that all such acts are a violation of personhood, for they mark a breach of right human relations, a transgression of a human covenant and an infraction of the command to love. The person immediately violated, of course, is the victim, for whom a sexual indiscretion entails the violation of bodily integrity, the right to establish physical boundaries and to choose what is done to one's body and by one's body.[20] In addition, sexual misconduct violates the personhood of the victim's spouse as well as the perpetrator's spouse.

In this chapter, however, we moved to a deeper violation inherent in this problem. Sexual misconduct is also a distortion of our human sexuality; it is antithetical to God's intention in creating us as sexual beings. For this reason, it is a betrayal of sexual trust. For the offending pastor, the betrayal runs deep, encompassing even a violation of his calling to live before the community in sexual integrity, whether he be single or married. The foundation for overcoming the problem of clergy sexual misconduct lies with a renewed commitment to living out the implications of the biblical understanding of human sexuality. As Charles Rassieur notes, "More apparent than anything else is the need for parish pastors to integrate their intellectual theology with their visceral humanity."[21]

Inherent in every act of clergy sexual indiscretion is another aspect as well. It is a betrayal of trust in the dimension of power. No attempt to reflect theologically on the phenomenon of clergy sexual misconduct is complete without considering this aspect.

4

Misconduct as Betrayal of a Power Trust

R ecent studies of the phenomenon of clergy sexual misconduct point out that because sexual liaisons between pastor and congregant involve power, they also constitute an abuse of power. In fact, a growing tide of opinion views clergy sexual misconduct chiefly, if not solely, as a violation of power, rather than a transgression of sexual norms. John Vogelsang declares that the problem "is less about sex and more about power. It has less to do with sexual misconduct such as adultery, and more to do with exploiting one's professional position for personal gain."[1]

Similarly Pamela Cooper-White writes, "We need nothing less than a total paradigm shift: we need to stop treating the problem as only one of sexual morality, emotional instability or addiction, and address the power dynamics of these mostly hidden abuses. Only when this happens and the church stops engaging in denial and collusion can the church be a place of authentic power, healing and proclamation for both women and men."[2]

In chapter three we viewed clergy sexual misconduct as a betrayal of a sexual trust. We argued that only by acknowledging the sexual violation involved can we lay a proper ethical foundation for dealing with the problem. This emphasis puts us at odds with those who minimize the dimension of sexual transgression we find present in clergy misconduct. At the same time, however, we agree with contemporary thinkers that misconduct is not merely a sexual transgression. It involves a violation of power.

We maintain that the two aspects are linked: Clergy sexual misconduct is simultaneously a sexual transgression and an abuse of power. It is a betrayal of trust both in the dimension of human sexuality and in the clergy-congregant relationship. In this chapter we view the latter aspect, seeing clergy sexual misconduct as an insidious betrayal of trust in the realm of power, a violation of the clergy position.

At first glance, the conjecture that a minister is susceptible to abusing power may appear incredible. Most pastors do not see themselves as wielders of power in the church. The idea of a powerful pastor is incongruous with the widely held picture of the Christlike minister who has renounced the use of power to become a servant to the "flock of God."

The image of the powerful minister also runs counter to the experience of most pastors, who see themselves as relatively powerless. One of the frustrations clergy consistently report is their inability to effect change in the church or in the lives of congregants despite the great amount of energy they expend in the attempt. Bill Schmidt sums up the attitude of many: "Pastoral caregivers often deny that they carry any power, or that power agendas operate in all human transactions. After all, we as pastoral caregivers are 'servants' of the people of God, and often feel powerless to positively affect the dilemmas of our parishioners' and counselees' lives."[3]

Despite their perception of the nature of the clergy office and in contrast to what they often experience in congregational life, pastors do command great power. For this reason they are vulnerable to misusing that power in many ways, including through sexual misconduct.

Power, Authority and Leadership

Gary A. Yukl maintains that "the essence of leadership is influence over followers."[4] Such influence is generally a predicate of authority and power, which in the church is connected to the ordained office. To see in what sense clergy sexual misconduct is an abuse of power, we must understand the reality of both power and authority as they operate in human relationships and then explore how ministers as church leaders embody spiritual authority and therefore command power.

Authority entails "the right to command, enforce obedience, make decisions"[5] or "the right to act by virtue of office, station or relation."[6] *Power,* in contrast, is the "ability to act so as to produce some change or bring about some event"[7] or the "capacity to exercise control."[8] In the context of interpersonal relations power refers to "an agent's potential influence over the attitudes and behavior of one or more designated target persons."[9] Or as Max Weber declared in his classic definition, power is "the possibility of imposing one's own will upon the behavior of other persons."[10]

So power is the potential for affecting the thinking, attitudes or conduct of another. Power, therefore, focuses on *ability* to influence others, whereas authority has to do with the *right* to exercise power.[11] For this reason, authority generally precedes power.

Persons in leadership positions in human institutions possess a certain inherent authority. As a result, in their relationships with others they command the power connected with this authority. The authority of leaders is connected to their symbolic function. Leaders stand as symbols of the ideals of the institution. They embody its collective identity and continuity, as well as its values, vision and mandate.

In addition to possessing this "authority of position," a leader may also command "person power." This power finds its source in the leader's own charismatic qualities and personal relationships with others in the institution.[12]

The Power of the Pastorate

Pastors, like other institutional leaders, function as symbols.[13] They embody the collective identity, as well as the values and vision of the community they represent—the church. As a result, people respond to pastors, whether unconsciously or consciously, in ways associated with the symbolic function they believe inheres in the ordained office.

Symbols play an important role in our lives. The theologian Paul Tillich theorizes that the potency of a symbol lies not only in its ability to point beyond itself but in the fact that it participates in the reality to which it points. Thereby a symbol is able to open up levels of reality that otherwise are closed to us and to unlock aspects of our inner being which correspond to that reality.[14] In short, to the person for whom the symbol is meaningful, it communicates something of a transcendent reality.

Many people perceive a pastor—by virtue of his office and apart from his own person—as a religious symbol. To them, a minister represents religious truth, the spiritual way of life and perhaps even the reality of God. As David Switzer notes, "The minister is a physical representation of the whole community of faith, of the tradition, of a way of viewing the meaning of life, of the dynamic power of faith, and of God Himself."[15] This symbolic aspect endows a minister with great spiritual authority.

The authority of the clergy as a symbolic office means that pastors command power to an extent that they may not fully realize. Ministers have at their disposal not only the power of their own presence as persons but also the power others associate with moral, religious or spiritual authority. They embody the authority of the church and even the authority of God.

Simply by appearing as a person wedded to a sacred vocation, a minister can mediate to others the presence of the eternal within the temporal, the infinite within the finite, the unchanging within the transient. For them, a pastor's presence mediates a certain sense of the holy and the transcendent in the midst of the mundane reality of life. A minister is able to weave into life a thread of meaning that can transform day-to-day acts into a coherent process. Switzer offers a helpful description of this capability: "The very physical presence of the minister has the power to stimulate those internal images, which through early learning in a highly emotionally charged relationship of dependence, have become a part of an individual's intrapersonal dynamics."[16]

Connected to the power of the pastorate as derived from its inherent symbolic function is the power of influence. A minister has the ability to affect the attitudes and behavior of others without the use of overt physical force. This special power is invested in pastors by those to whom they minister.

A pastor's power of influence is linked to the role of spiritual professional. It resembles what occurs in any professional-client relationship. Clients seek out a practitioner when they are experiencing problems or needs for which they lack the expertise. When they perceive that their needs are spiritual, many people look to the spiritual professional—their pastor. Congregants approach the minister rather than another church member because they believe that his training, experience and role in the congregation place him in a position to assist them. They assume that he possesses the prerequisite knowledge and necessary skills to meet the need posed by the situation.

People who seek the expertise of professional practitioners invest them with a special power of influence. They allow professional caregivers to diagnose the situation and to suggest appropriate ways of responding to it. Power of influence, therefore, is always ascribed by the client to the practitioner. As Karen Lebacqz indicates, this power entrusts professional caregivers with immense influence: "the power to define our needs and problems as well as to respond to them. And with the power of definition comes a significant control over our lives."[17]

Some congregants relate to their pastor in a similar manner. In so far as they look to him as a spiritual professional, they invest him with a similar power of influence. They give him the power to name their need and to suggest appropriate courses of action. Because they believe that as their spiritual physician "the pastor knows best," these congregants readily accept his diagnosis of their spiritual ailments and are predisposed to follow his prescriptions for their cure.

Certain congregants likewise place immense power of influence in their minister because of his function in the congregation. As the spiritual "shepherd" of "God's flock" a pastor often has a special role in the lives of those to whom he ministers. Many congregants look to their pastor as the one who above all others will provide the spiritual care they need. Some assume that their minister will always act in their best interests, even to the extent of setting aside his own needs for the sake of service to the congregation.

Congregants who look to their pastor as a self-sacrificing spiritual caregiver grant him an influence over their own personal lives and conduct not given to colleagues, friends or even family members. And these people allow themselves to be vulnerable to their pastor, especially in crisis situations.

Because they trust their pastor, many congregants are willing to invest in him a degree of power they deny to others. They believe that a minister will use this power and influence only for their good. They are confident that he would never intentionally hurt a person under his care. These congregants assume that their pastor will always view the power they entrust to him as a sacred trust.

Vulnerability and Abuse

In the situations they confront in life, many congregants allow themselves to become vulnerable to their pastor in various ways. Because of the nature of the pastoral office, from time to time (such as when they encounter the loss of a loved one or seek counseling from him) they enter into a special intimacy with their minister. This is not the natural intimacy connected with the bond between child and parent, nor the voluntary intimacy shared between friends or spouses. It is similar instead to the intimacy a client gives to a professional practitioner for the purpose of securing some benefit (such as physical health in the case of a medical doctor).[18]

Rather than being reciprocal as in natural or voluntary intimacy, the relationship between professional and client is one-sided. Professionals see clients in an office rather than in their homes. The client shares with the professional personal information—preferably all the details relevant to the situation. But this sharing is not reciprocated. As a result, the client is vulnerable in a manner that the professional is not.

Congregants who turn to their pastor for spiritual comfort or direction step into the realm of one-sided intimacy with him. They become vulnerable, entrusting to the minister the power of influence, with the anticipation that he will become an agent of God's provision for their need.

Every situation of vulnerability involves risk. The possession of power can lead to the abuse of power. And the person to whom we entrust ourselves may violate that trust. So also a pastor can use his influence over others and the vulnerability of his congregants to promote selfish ends. If a minister exploits the power and privilege of this office to gain personal advantage, he abuses the power of the ordained position.[19]

When the vulnerability of congregant to pastor extends to the sexual dimension, the situation is ripe for a grave abuse of power. If a pastor redirects the power a congregant has entrusted to him toward his own sexual gratification, he has crossed the line into clergy sexual misconduct.[20]

The potential for an abuse of power in the sexual realm arises from the special nature of sexual vulnerability. In no aspect of human existence are we more vulnerable than in the sexual dimension. Because of the connection between sexuality and our incompleteness as embodied beings, being vulnerable is part of the essential dynamic of sexually. It is in sexual relationships that our fragility, insecurity and need to feel accepted, which often lie buried deep within ourselves, come to the surface. In a nurturing relationship, our vulnerability, including its sexual dimension, can open the way for God to foster growth within us. However, when someone to whom we entrusted our vulnerability takes advantage of his power over us for personal gain, we receive wounds that go deep into our being.

The violation of vulnerability involved in an abuse of power in the sexual sphere makes it especially insidious. As Peter Rutter declares, a female congregant brings into the pastor-congregant relationship her "intimate, wounded, vulnerable, or undeveloped parts" which he holds in trust.[21] These dimensions are often closely tied to her sexuality. Her wounds may include sexual or psychological trauma dating back to childhood or a history of being treated as a sexual object.

Whatever caused her woundedness, she may seek out her pastor, hoping to find acceptance and self-worth as a person. Through a healthy relationship with him, she desires to gain healing and a new sense of wholeness. As she senses a special connection to her pastor, she may reveal increasingly more of herself to him, adding to her vulnerability. Eventually the conditioning produced by earlier experiences of sexual exploitation may make her open to maintaining her relationship to this powerful man on sexual terms, if she senses that he desires or demands it. In this situation, Rutter asserts, "even a woman with a firm sense of boundaries in other kinds of relationships may well stop guarding them so that her core may be seen and known by this man."[22] She may agree to sexual contact hoping to insure the relationship with her pastor.

A minister who moves their relationship into the sexual sphere may be motivated by his own needs. He may hope to find his own personal healing through the act. Whatever his motivation, through sexual contact he has in fact exploited her vulnerability. He has violated the trust she placed in him as her pastor, yielding to his own desires or needs at her expense. Drawing from Rutter, Karen Lebacqz and Ronald Barton conclude that the sexual contact "revictimizes her, repeating patterns from her past, and keeps her from recognizing and claiming her own strength apart from a man."[23]

Sexual Contact and Mutual Consent

This scenario describes many situations of clergy sexual abuse. But does it encompass all sexual encounters between a pastor and a congregant? Occasionally a congregant initiates sexual contact with her pastor. Or sexual activity may occur with what appears to be the full consent of both persons. What then? Does *every* sexual act between a congregant and her pastor entail an abuse of power and a betrayal of trust?

While acknowledging that these situations do arise, most contemporary thinkers maintain that any sexual contact between pastor and congregant does entail an abuse of power. Marie Fortune offers this assessment:

> It is certainly not unusual for a parishioner to be attracted to her minister. Ministers frequently appear to embody those attractive qualities that may be missing in a person's relational life. The parishioner may in fact be

attracted to the power of the role itself. But the pastor who responds affirmatively to a sexual initiative by a parishioner allows the boundaries of the pastoral relationship to be broken. The pastor has the power and the responsibility to maintain these boundaries in order to preserve the pastoral relationship. This serves the best interest of the parishioner *and* the best interests of the pastor.[24]

Peter Rutter is equally adamant. He declares in no uncertain terms that "*any sexual behavior by a man in power within what I define as the forbidden zone is inherently exploitative of a woman's trust.* Because he is the keeper of that trust, it is the man's responsibility, *no matter what the level of provocation or apparent consent by the woman,* to assure that sexual behavior does not take place."[25]

Ruth Tiffany Barnhouse agrees.

Male clergy need to realize that a woman's "consent" is not enough. Congregations abound with lonely women, both married and single. Many of these will at least yield to, if not actually solicit, sexual attentions from clergy in order to get some companionship. Some behave this way because the culture has trained them to believe it is the only way to get serious attention from men. Others do so out of a naive belief that *other* men might take advantage of them but clergy certainly would not. It should be realized that it is impossible, even with the best will in the world, *not* to take advantage of women who are sexually compliant for such reasons.[26]

The uncompromising position voiced by Fortune, Rutter and Barnhouse seems especially applicable in cases when a congregant initiates sexual contact. In such a situation the woman's advance does not discharge the pastor from his role as the one responsible to maintain the boundaries. The wise pastor realizes that there are likely deeper dynamics at work when a congregant under his care offers herself to him sexually. The congregant's actual goal in the act may be to guarantee that she will be accepted and treated as someone special. Her offer of sexual contact could well be the only means she knows to maintain a relationship with a man she has come to value.[27]

But are there not cases in which both persons consent to the relationship?

What about a situation in which the pastor and the congregant fall in love and consequently engage in sex?

Contemporary thinkers deny that mutual consent is possible in a relationship involving a minister and a congregant. They say that the pastor-congregant role excludes the possibility of mutual consent because of its inherent inequality. As Marie Fortune explains, meaningful consent "requires full knowledge *and* the power to say 'no.' "[28] This necessitates that the two persons meet in a situation of equality. But given the inherent and ascribed power of the pastorate and the congregant's state of vulnerability, the pastor-congregant relationship entails an imbalance of power. This power differential is inevitably transferred to the sexual dimension.

Many considerations may motivate a congregant to become involved sexually with her pastor. She may fear the loss of the pastoral relationship. She may be misinformed about his intentions. Or she may have found his attention comforting during the crisis which originally led her to him.[29] Whatever her motivation, the congregant enters the relationship with a special vulnerability that her pastor does not reciprocate. So she is in an unequal position relative to him.

Marie Fortune describes the difficulty involved: "A counseling relationship is by definition a relationship of unequal power in which the needs of the client/parishioner are the priority. A love/sexual relationship is an ideally mutual and equal relationship intended to meet the needs of both persons involved."[30] A sexual relationship involving a congregant and her pastor is illegitimate, therefore, because it creates what Fortune and other thinkers call "dual relationships."[31] In this sense, sexual contact between a minister and a congregant is similar to any such contact involving a client and a professional caregiver—whether doctor, psychiatrist or counselor.

Because the vulnerability of the congregant precludes the aspect of equality essential to mutual consent, a liaison involving a pastor and a congregant is never sex between two consenting persons. For this reason, a pastor-congregant sexual relationship differs significantly from an affair involving two church members.

Three Abuses of Power

In his monumental study *The Anatomy of Power,* John Kenneth Galbraith pinpoints three ways in which power is exercised in human relationships. He differentiates among condign, compensatory and conditioned power.[32] *Condign power* is the process of influencing others by threatening adverse consequences. In Galbraith's words, it "wins submission by the ability to impose an alternative to the preferences of the individual or group that is sufficiently unpleasant or painful so that these preferences are abandoned."[33] *Compensatory power* moves in the opposite direction. It is the process of influencing others by offering affirmative reward, something the individual or group values. *Conditioned power,* in contrast, operates through the belief structures of its targets: "persuasion, education, or the social commitment to what seems natural, proper, or right causes the individual to submit to the will of another or of others."[34] The clergy-congregant relationship is susceptible to the abuse of each aspect of power Galbraith delineates.

The situation of dependency in which the congregant's need and vulnerability place her leaves her open to being controlled by the threat of adverse consequences. Her pastor abuses his *condign power* if he cajoles her into sexual activity by threatening to sever the relationship.

Similarly, the congregant's anticipation of the positive benefits she could gain through the relationship with her pastor makes her susceptible to being controlled by the offer of reward. The pastor abuses the *compensatory power* he possesses when he convinces her that by responding to his sexual advances she can obtain the fulfillment of her hopes.

The clergy-congregant relationship is especially susceptible to an abuse of conditioned power. A congregant generally enters the relationship believing that her pastor would never suggest any activity that would be morally wrong or would violate her in any way. A pastor abuses his *conditioned power* when her ingrained assumption of his integrity allows him to overcome her inhibitions and submit her to his sexual advances.

Sexual contact does not always entail an overt abuse of power on the part of the pastor. Occasionally it comes at the initiative of the congregant as an outworking of her misperceptions about the situation. Fearing that she may lose the man who holds such promise for healing from her wounds, she may attempt to maintain the relationship through sexual contact. Or motivated by unrealistic expectations of the benefits, the congregant may be the one to initiate sexual contact.

On the basis of our previous discussion, we must conclude that even when the congregant initiates sexual contact, the pastor's complicity constitutes an abuse of power. Not only does he abandon the professional relationship, he also misunderstands her motivations. The pastor fails to perceive that she was actually asking for acceptance and seeking to maintain the relationship, perhaps in accordance with the way she has been conditioned to relate to powerful men. By cooperating in her destructive pattern of conduct, the pastor abuses the consign and compensatory power that she has entrusted to him because of his position. Rather than clarifying the situation for her, he has victimized her.

Regardless of who initiates sexual contact, the introduction of sexual behavior into the minister-congregant relationship violates a sacred trust. It exploits the power and influence a pastor enjoys by virtue of the clergy office. And it preys on the vulnerability of a person who has placed herself under his care.

For this reason, Don Basham is correct in exclaiming, "A minister's position of unique privilege is also a position of unique peril!"[35] The pastoral office does involve risks. A minister is susceptible to the sexual approach of a congregant, or to accusations of misconduct or misuse of pastoral power to meet personal needs. Despite the pastor's susceptibility, however, only the congregant is vulnerable. Marie Fortune explains: "Parishioners look to a pastor to meet their needs for guidance, counsel, support, and care. In seeking help from someone who is a designated authority, who offers to provide these services, and who holds power, parishioners are vulnerable and thus able to be harmed or taken advantage of."[36] The greatest risk for the minister, then, is to fall into the trap of abusing the sacred trust of others and exploiting the power of his position for personal gain and advantage.

Clergy sexual misconduct is a grave breach of the trust within the pastor-congregant relationship. It is an abuse of the power of the ordained office. At the same time, this abuse of power leads to a violation of the dynamic of personhood in which clergy play a significant role. This violation works in many directions. Of these three loom most crucial: violation of the congregant as a person, violation of the pastoral identity and violation of the divine image.

Abuse as Violation of the Congregant

Obviously clergy sexual misconduct constitutes a violation of the person of the congregant involved in the act. Through sexual contact, the offending pastor has abused the power over her person that she entrusted to him.

Psychologists remind us that crucial to one's sense of personhood is the establishment of clear "boundaries." That is, we gain our identity in part when we learn to sense where "I" end and "you" begin. Healthy relationships contribute to the sense of personhood in each person involved. They provide self-defining experiences, experiences that encourage the development of clear, yet flexible, personal boundaries. Healthy relationships also provide experiences that lead to effective and helpful ways of interacting with one another on the basis of a clear sense of our own personhood.[37]

When our sense of personal boundaries is fuzzy, however, or when we sense that someone has encroached on our personhood by transgressing our personal boundary, we become confused. Our sense of boundaries is especially crucial in the sexual dimension. Almost instinctively we protect this vulnerable aspect of our person from intrusion.

Cognizant of the importance of inviolate personal sexual boundaries, our society acknowledges that any overstepping of them constitutes abuse. Sexual abuse may even take the seemingly harmless form of verbal innuendos or crude jokes. People are increasingly less willing to tolerate sexual talk within inappropriate relationships, such as among work colleagues. Verbal boundary violation is one form of sexual abuse.

The work of professional caregivers, however, often requires a certain blurring of normal personal boundaries. Hence, the patient-physician relationship allows for physical contact which in other contexts is deemed a violation of the patient's physical boundary. Similarly, a psychiatrist may cross a sensitive psychological boundary of the counselee in a manner that is illegitimate in any other context. As Schmidt notes, "the therapeutic process, by its very nature, invites the blurring of normal boundaries."[38]

Pastoral care also involves an occasional blurring of boundaries. In the presence of a caring pastor a congregant may, for perhaps the first time, find the freedom to let down her carefully constructed, defensive and rigid boundaries so she can find healing. Her openness, however, may awaken deep sexual feelings in the pastor. Schmidt pinpoints the dynamic at work: "It becomes seductive for us as caregivers when another 'hands over' the maintenance of their lives to us."[39]

But the congregant has not placed herself in the care of her pastor to assuage sexual gratification. What she desires is healing of the wounds that led her to construct rigid personal boundaries in other relationships. Only then can she gain the wholeness and sense of true personal boundaries that facilitates reciprocal male-female intimacy.

When a pastor yields to the seduction her vulnerability awakens in him, he could abuse his power and violate her person. His sexual advance constitutes an immediate violation of her person, for to transgress her personal sexual boundary would be to take advantage of his pastoral knowledge of her blurred boundaries. In addition to its immediate effects, sexual contact also marks a violation of her person over the longer term. Rather than promoting her healing and her ability to establish a sense of personal wholeness through healthy boundaries, his sexual advance would inflict additional wounds in her already fragile self-awareness.

Because of the potential for abuse that results from any blurring of boundaries, the pastor must be constantly sensitive to the personal boundaries of others.

Abuse as the Violation of the Pastoral Identity

The person whose identity is most obviously violated through clergy sexual misconduct is the congregant who entered the relationship with the hope of being healed. Often overlooked is the violation of the pastor's identity that results from this type of abuse of power.

All persons receive some sense of personal identity from the work they do. Those who view themselves as merely employees of a company are generally well practiced in the art of separating themselves from their role on the job. They view their work as but one of several dimensions of existence which comprise their identity. People in the helping professions, in contrast, find a greater degree of their sense of self linked to their professional role.

This is especially the case with pastors, who often nearly equate their personal identity with their vocation as an ordained minister of the church. David K. Switzer provides this vivid description of the close link between the pastoral office and the personal identity of the minister: "Most ministers not only *work* at their profession, and invest time and energy, but at the core of the self is 'minister,' a bound collection of self-images, values, faith, and commitments—a person who has responded and *is responding* to a vocation, not just one who has chosen an occupation. I do not just *perform* a ministry, I *am* a minister."[40]

While it may boost the minister's self-image as a truly dedicated pastor, the close connection between the pastoral role and the minister's personal identity also entails risks. Specifically, it increases the risk of clergy sexual misconduct, which violates, and even destroys, the minister's pastoral identity.

Sexual abuse belies and jeopardizes a pastor's profession. An identity-destroying act of sexual contact with a congregant may arise in quite different contexts. Sexual misconduct is likely to occur when a pastor is struggling with low self-esteem and a sense of personal failure.

Our human dependence on others for our sense of self makes us all susceptible to seeking self-validation in socially or ethically unacceptable ways. Schmidt describes the psychological dynamic involved: "All of our identities, both personal and professional, are sustained by the mirroring response of others. We all seek confirmation of who we are. This is appropriate and necessary. However, we may live out this need in the form of a narcissistic vulnerability in which we attempt to compensate for our woundedness by exaggerated efforts at self-enhancement."[41]

The pastor experiencing an identity crisis is not immune from falling into this downward spiral. Like other practitioners who derive their identity from their vocation, he may quite naturally look to his professional role for validation of his person. He may seek to find his personal identity through his activities as a professional minister. And he may attempt to compensate for his personal insecurity through his pastoral work. The wounded pastor is especially susceptible to the temptation to use the power of his office to bolster his flagging sense of self.

One additional dynamic makes his search for identity highly explosive. In our culture, males tend to seek healing from woundedness and discover personal identity through sexual contact.[42] This tendency is augmented by the myth widely propagated in our society that an individual must be genitally active to be a full person. Influenced by this cultural dynamic, the wounded pastor may consider using his pastoral role to find sexual acceptance from a vulnerable woman under his care.

Despite his expectations, a sexual encounter with a congregant cannot provide the sense of self the pastor truly needs, just as it cannot fulfill her hope for healing. Rather than obtaining the personal identity he is seeking, the pastor engages in an abuse of power which violates his pastoral identity. His action indicates that he is not serving as the caring pastor he desires to be. Rather than bolstering his sense of self, he has actually diminished his image as a professional in the eyes of others and in his own eyes as well.

Sexual abuse only compounds the problems a pastor expects to cure through an affair. While low self-esteem opens a minister to an ill-fated attempt to discover personal identity through sexual contact with a congregant, success as a pastor may likewise create a context for clergy sexual misconduct. The research of Dean Ludwig and Clinton Longenecker into successful business leaders provides insight into this.

Ludwig and Longenecker discovered that success places a business leader in a privileged position within the organization. They offer four characteristics of this position: "First, personal and organizational success often allows leaders to become complacent and lose strategic focus, diverting attention to things other than the management of their organization. Second, success often leads to privileged access to information, people, or objects. Third, success often leads to unrestrained control of organizational resources. Fourth, success can inflate a leader's belief in his or her personal ability to manipulate or control outcomes."[43]

The privileged position itself entails a special temptation for business leaders; it places them in a context in which unethical activity could readily occur. Ludwig and Longenecker remark, "Even individuals with a highly developed moral sense can be challenged (tempted?) by the 'opportunities' resulting from the convergence of these four dynamics."[44] Specifically, "when loss of strategic focus is coupled with privileged access," business leaders may succumb to the temptation to use their position and status "to promote nonstrategic, non-organizational purposes."[45]

The potential for abuse of position is augmented, however, by the negative side effects of success. Ludwig and Longenecker assert that successful leaders can become emotionally expansive, developing an insatiable appetite for success, thrill, gratification and control. Because the price of success is often isolation from spouse, family, friends and peers, successful leaders can be also plagued by a lack of intimacy in their lives. In addition, success often engenders anxiety and increased stress, produced by the growing, gnawing fear of failure. Finally, successful leaders may experience the "emptiness syndrome." No longer finding personal meaning in the vocation which once was theirs, they now seek other ways to satisfy their need for meaning. Ludwig and Longenecker conclude that when these negative byproducts of success combine with the leader's privileged position, "they create a rather potent combination for unethical behavior on the part of the successful leader."[46]

The experience of the successful pastor often mirrors that of the business leader. Perhaps to an even greater extent than his counterpart in the business community, the effective pastor enjoys a privileged position in the church. In fact, prominence generally comes to business leaders only as the fruit of years of diligent work in a competitive environment. Because of the significance of his ordained office, in contrast, the pastor may enjoy privilege almost immediately, which his success only serves to augment.

At the same time, the effective pastor may encounter similar negative by-products of success. He too is susceptible to loss of meaning in his vocation. Like other successful people, he may also come to desire the experience of new thrills. And because of the long hours demanded by the ministry, the successful pastor, like his business counterpart, may grow distant from those persons with whom he should be enjoying intimacy. Especially vulnerable to deterioration is his marital relationship. The loss of intimacy with his wife only compounds his growing inner frustration in the face of outward success. So the successful pastor, like the business leader, may find himself in the midst of a "midlife crisis."

The search for new meaning, the desire for excitement and the unmet need for intimacy may raise in the mind of the successful pastor thoughts of a sexual encounter. His privileged position in the church allows access to such an encounter. Through the routine activities as a functioning pastor he will come in contact with vulnerable women who find him and his success attractive. The effective pastor seeking to cope with midlife dissatisfaction and the vulnerable woman seeking to find healing through a relationship constitute an explosive situation. The pastor may come to believe that an adulterous relationship promises a cure for his midlife crisis.[47]

The pastor may engage in sexual misconduct because he expects the relationship with the congregant to offer renewed meaning, vitality or personal intimacy. But the sexual liaison cannot fulfill his needs. As Ruth Tiffany Barnhouse concludes, "The clergyman may see the woman involved as a gift of God to relieve his misery. This is *never* true. She is actually being *used* to put off the necessity of squarely facing the real problem."[48]

Regardless of his intentions and anticipations, a successful pastor's sexual misconduct constitutes an abuse of power which violates his pastoral identity. In entering into a sexual relationship with a congregant, the minister is dissipating the power associated with his privileged position in an ill-fated search for a renewed sense of personal identity. As a pastor, however, his calling is to use the power of the ordained position for the benefit of others. By inappropriately engaging in the sexual act, he is denying his calling. He violates his sacred trust both by the selfish misuse of his power and by the additional wound his act inflicts on the congregant who entered into a relationship with her pastor hoping to experience healing. He may enter into a sexual liaison anticipating that contact with a congregant will bring positive results, but his sexual misconduct only serves to efface his identity as a minister of the gospel.

Sexual abuse undermines a pastor's usefulness to his flock. Finally, clergy sexual misconduct violates the pastor's own identity because it undermines his vocation as a facilitator of growth in the lives of his congregants. The ultimate goal in any pastor-congregant relationship is to foster spiritual growth in both persons, but especially the church member.

We experience spiritual growth in many ways. But one crucial means that the Holy Spirit uses in producing growth in us is personal relationships with others. Contemporary psychologists remind us of the importance of other people for personal identity formation. We discover ourselves and create our sense of identity in person-to-person relationships. But in addition, through other people we discover God. God is personal, and for that reason, we come to know dimensions of our personal God as we encounter God in others.

As we noted earlier in this chapter, for many congregants no one is more significant as a symbol of the personal God than their pastor. For this reason they place a great trust in their minister. Some congregants believe that he will consistently seek to be a means whereby they might encounter God and that he will never willfully act in a manner that will present a false image of God's nature.

In the previous chapter we noted that God intends that human sexuality reflect God's holy character and that our sexual conduct is an indication of our understanding of God's relationship to us. This indicates how sexual relations between pastor and congregant violate the pastoral identity. A minister is called to enter into relationships with others in a manner that allows them to gain insight into the nature of God. This is especially important in the sexual dimension. When the pastor is characterized by purity and fidelity, his life proclaims God's fidelity toward humans. A sexual liaison with a congregant, in contrast, mars the pastoral identity. In her relationship with her pastor, the wounded congregant no longer experiences the fidelity of the holy God. The sexual contact has destroyed the pastor-congregant relationship as a means for the activity of the Holy Spirit in constructing mature Christian personhood.

Abuse as a Violation of the Divine Image

A sexual liaison within the pastor-congregant relationship is a violation of personhood of both the vulnerable woman and the identity-seeking minister. But an additional violation of personhood directly links our discussion of power with the understanding of sexuality set forth in the previous chapter. Sexual misconduct of any kind is a violation of human personhood as the image of God. When the act is perpetrated by a pastor, the violation also includes the abuse of the power inherent in the ordained office.

Central to the Christian faith is the biblical declaration that humans are the image of God (Genesis 1:26). The Scriptures indicate that God created us with a special task, namely, that we be the divine image-bearers, who care for his creation just as God cares for us (Genesis 2:15).

For the historical foundation for the designation "image of God," contemporary biblical scholars draw from the practice among kings of the ancient Near East of constructing images of themselves in territories where they could not be present in person. Such images served to represent their majesty and power.[49] We are the image of God insofar as we represent the Creator to creation, that is, as we mirror God's own nature to the people around us.

The Bible likewise presents the image of God as a social rather than merely an individual reality. According to the first creation narrative, God created male and female in the image of God. The Creator's purpose was that humans enjoy fellowship or "community" with each other. More specifically, the second narrative suggests that the creation of the woman delivered the man from his isolation. The biblical understanding of the purpose of our creation means that the divine image is a shared, corporate reality, which is fully present only in community.[50] So it is primarily within relationships that we are the image of God.

Both the reflective and the corporate aspects of the divine image ultimately come from the Christian understanding of God as triune. Throughout eternity God is the loving fellowship of the three persons who comprise the one God. The creation of humankind in the divine image means that we are to express the relational dynamic of the triune God. But we can show the relational reality of God only within loving relationships. As we experience true fellowship in community with others, we reflect God's own character, which is love. And as we reflect the divine essence (love), we find our true identity.

The Bible teaches that God is characterized by a special kind of love. God is that self-giving love which seeks the benefit of the other even if it means personal loss. We see this love in the story of Jesus. As Paul says, "Though he was rich, yet for your sakes he became poor, so that you through his poverty might become rich" (2 Corinthians 8:9). This divine love stands as a stark contrast to worldly love. Rather than being unconditional, worldly love is aroused by the beauty of the beloved, fulfills certain needs in the lover and provides the lover with satisfaction or enjoyment.[51] Classically Christian thinkers have characterized this contrast by differentiating between *agapē* (self-giving love) and *eros* (love aroused by the desire to possess the beloved).

Human relationships that reflect the reality of God are those in which agape is prominent. Relationships founded solely on eros, in contrast, blur our understanding of God's character and therefore distort the divine image. The sexual dimension of human existence is especially susceptible to the triumph of eros over agape, and therefore, in this area, humans tend often to distort the image of God.

Loving relationships occur in various contexts of human life. But above all, God intends that Christ's disciples resemble the fellowship which characterizes the trinitarian Persons. God desires that the church strive to be the community of love, in order to show God's love to all creation. From this divine intent, the church derives its identity and believers find true person-hood as Christ's disciples.

The fundamental purpose of the ordained office, in turn, lies in its role of helping the church obey its mandate to be God's people for the sake of the world. The pastor's calling includes serving as an example and a shepherd to the flock of God, so that the church might grow in grace and reflect to an increasing extent God's character.

Cognizant of the holy calling of the ordained office, congregants invest in their pastor a special power and influence—a special trust. Congregants look to their pastor to exemplify the love that characterizes God. They anticipate that the pastor's relationships with his congregants will provide a living model for them to emulate. They expect the pastor to be a picture of true Christian personhood as the image of God.

An unavoidable dimension of eros is operative in almost every act of sexual intercourse. When the sex act occurs within its proper context, agape is present with eros. Kept within the boundaries of agape, the element of eros can be wholesome and enhance the pleasure of the partners. At the same time, the presence of eros means that any sexual relationship runs the danger that the partners may allow eros to crowd out agape. When this happens, the relationship cannot reflect God's self-giving love, and the partners' sexual liaison has violated their personhood as the image of God.

Any illicit sexual relationship, therefore, mars the divine image. Because of the special trust invested in the ordained office, however, when the liaison involves a pastor and a congregant, the sexual misconduct takes on an additional dimension.

As we have noted, God intends that pastors guide the church in being a people who live as the image of God. Congregants entrust great power to their pastor, anticipating that he will diligently seek to model God's self-giving love in the minister's relationships with them. But a pastor is also susceptible to using the power a congregant invests in him for his own personal advantage. When a minister is sexually attracted to a congregant, he enters a realm of special danger and grave temptation. He may fall prey to abusing the power the situation bestows on him and seek to transform a relationship which God intends to model agape into one ruled by eros. Sexual contact in such a context marks the victory of the desire to possess the other (eros) over the commitment to self-sacrifice for the sake of the other (agape). A sexual liaison between the pastor and the congregant violates their personhood as the image of God. But, in addition, the act undermines the integrity of his pastorate, marring what God designed to be a model of the divine image.

All occasions of clergy sexual misconduct entail a violation of the integrity of the pastorate. The perpetrator has betrayed the trust between pastor and people. In so doing, he has implicitly violated his ordination vow. Because of the seriousness of this problem, the Christian community must work together in the various dimensions of dealing with it. These include engaging in healing ministries to the victims, setting forth effective strategies of prevention and developing appropriate measures for discipline and restoration of offenders. To these practical aspects of clergy sexual misconduct we now turn.

5
Ministering to the Victims of Misconduct

Frank was a gifted and able pastor who despite his relative youth had already gained national stature as an evangelical leader. His ministry focused on instructing other "full-time" Christian workers in ordering their lives and priorities for effectiveness in God's service. Of particular concern to him was to articulate a high biblical standard of marriage and family. Consequently, in his public ministry he idealized his own marriage and family in such a way that—perhaps unintentionally—he caused those who fell short of that standard to sense both guilt and shame.

Even as Frank was extolling Christian marriage, he was involved in an adulterous relationship. When his moral failure became public, it naturally created a sensation. Soon several prominent evangelical leaders from various parts of the United States who shared a concern for Frank's ministry rushed to his aid. In a hastily arranged hotel meeting, the ad hoc group confronted Frank with his sexual misconduct.

The young pastor responded in an exemplary manner. Within the sympathetic company of his friends, he acknowledged his personal guilt, accepted responsibility for his actions and wept tears of repentance. Pleased with this response, the evangelical leaders accepted the repentance of their fallen brother, extended God's promise of forgiveness to him and inaugurated a process of discipline. Within a year Frank officially reentered the gospel ministry through a public service of repentance and restoration. Today his ministry appears to be even more fruitful than it was before this tragic event.

The quick response of Frank's friends in salvaging his ministry is laudatory. Their willingness to confront him, hear his confession and walk with him through a process of discipline embodies true biblical compassion. And the rehabilitation of the offending pastor, symbolized by a beautiful public act of restoration, provides a model for others to follow.

But however beneficial the process may have proven for Frank and his ministry, it leaves gnawing questions unanswered. What led his friends to assume that they had the insight, skills and authority to deal with him? Why was the process of discipline and restoration completed with such speed? Why were the implications of adultery for Christian leadership—so important in the early church—lightly set aside? Why was the entire process dominated by the goal of salvaging Frank's ministry? Did the group seek to confront their friend with the deeper causes of his misconduct, including the unresolved issues in his life that could lead him to become a repeat offender? The single-minded focus on the restoration of a pastor led Frank's support group to avoid the wider ramifications of his sexual failure and largely ignore the other persons affected by his actions. In planning how best to confront Frank with his sin, they did not interview his wife. Nor did they give consideration to the implications of the problem for Frank's children. Most incredible of all, however, in their deliberations and subsequent plan of action they overlooked the woman with whom their friend had been sexually involved.

The focus on Frank and his ministry, together with the lack of attention given to his family and to the other woman involved, is paralleled by the all-male makeup of the deputation that confronted him. Not only did the group itself not question the lack of female representation, it produced little subsequent comment in the evangelical community. Yet this was one of the most serious limitations of the process. The absence of women meant that the group operated without a female perspective on the situation. Not only do oversights such as this set the stage for a biased hearing, they reinforce the myth of the seductive female who destroys the ministry of the vulnerable male pastor.

It is difficult to escape the conclusion that in the midst of their laudable intentions and exemplary action, Frank's friends viewed their brother primarily as the victim and not the victimizer. They seem to have operated—at least implicitly—from the widely held but often unstated assumption that the pastor who gets involved with a congregant has been victimized. People may believe that he was unwise, even impulsive, but ultimately they conclude that in a moment of weakness he succumbed to the temptation posed by a seductive woman. Viewing the pastor as the victim naturally leads us to set his rehabilitation as our highest priority.

We cannot deal constructively with clergy sexual misconduct, however, until we reject and reverse this deep-seated assumption. Rather than viewing the pastor as the victim and focusing our resources on the task of salvaging his ministry, we must identify the many victims of his sexual misconduct. In chapter one we noted that an incident of clergy sexual misconduct affects a variety of people. If we would respond properly to clergy sexual failure, we must minister to all who bear the effects of the unfortunate action, not just the pastor.

Ministry to persons touched by clergy sexual misconduct means helping them cope with the situation they now face. It includes helping them honestly appraise their own responsibility so that they may move from guilt to the experience of forgiveness and restoration. Further, we must assist them in moving from anger to forgiving the perpetrator(s) of whatever injury came their way. And we must help them pick up the pieces and get on with their lives.

Our ability to engage in this kind of ministry requires that our personal attitude toward the victims be set right. We must overcome our tendency to see them as the ones who were ultimately responsible for the pastor's action, and realize that they are the victims of clergy sexual misconduct.

The most obvious victim in clergy sexual misconduct is the congregant with whom the pastor became involved. Yet the victimized woman has traditionally been treated in a cavalier fashion. So often, she is dismissed from the scenario with apparently no consideration. But if we are to deal constructively in the wake of a pastor's sexual indiscretion, we must minister to the one whom he led across the forbidden zone.

Seductive Female or Vulnerable Woman?

> After introducing herself upon entering the counselor's office, Colleen lowered her head slightly and looked him intently in the eye in a manner that required no accompanying words. She then fluffed her hair, pulled her sweater tightly over her well-endowed figure, and looked at him again flirtatiously. The counselor sensed the powerful pull of Colleen's sexuality.[1]

The prevailing assumption among Christians pictures "the other woman," the congregant with whom a pastor becomes sexually involved, as an evil seductress. The Colleens of the world have evoked a vast body of literature warning pastors about the "seductive female." In one representative essay, marriage and family therapist Andre Bustanoby reviews the familiar strategies: the open-door policy (leaving his office door open during counseling sessions), referral and moving toward team counseling. He then speaks of the counselor's role in assisting the counselee in overcoming her tendency to use her sexuality to control men.[2]

Although Bustanoby claims that "pastors in large churches may encounter someone like Colleen as often as once a month,"[3] the truth is, the woman he describes rarely destroys a pastor's ministry. If her approach is as obvious as he depicts, no conscientious pastor would enter into a long-term counseling relationship with her, not merely because she is seductive but because to do so would be to take on a client whose emotional needs are beyond his skill level to help. The best assistance he can give the client who fits the description of the "seductive female" is to understand how vulnerable *she* is. The helpful pastor seeks to assist her in understanding how she became a self-defeating seductive female, while coming to grips himself with why she is sexually threatening. Behind Colleen's appearance is almost certainly a history of victimization and unhealthy relationships with men that goes back to childhood.

But supposing the unwary pastor is seduced by Colleen's sexual overtures. Does a woman with a broken past, who in her search for healing enters into a sexual relationship with a pastor, deserve to be treated as an outcast, responded to with contempt and thereby placed once again in jeopardy? Of course not, but this is often the tragic result.

Many Christians assume that only a Colleen would cross the forbidden zone with a pastor. Marie Fortune puts her finger on this tendency. In describing the responses to Peter Donovan's indiscretions, she concludes, "Too often the local church reacts much like family members to the revelation of incest."[4] We can hear the pain in her voice when she speaks on behalf of the "other women" in this situation: "I wanted the system to work for them, to make justice out of injustice, and I believed the church had the capacity to do this."[5] But instead she found "an institution totally unprepared and initially unwilling to protect its people from the actions of one of its designated leaders."[6]

Until this mindset changes, the most victimized person of clergy sexual failure will continue to be the other woman. Of course, in certain cases she may bear some responsibility. But as long as we simply assume that this woman is a seductress and the primary cause of the pastor's downfall, we will not be able to address the crucial underlying problems.

Ministering to victimized congregants requires that we understand why a congregant would enter into a sexual relationship with her pastor. Who is vulnerable? Why is she at risk? What kind of woman is susceptible?

J. Steven Muse pinpoints four general types of vulnerable women.[7] The first is what he calls the "primarily healthy" woman. She is not struggling with deep-seated wounds derived from an unfortunate past but is undergoing a personal crisis. In the midst of this crisis, she finds in the pastor "the strong and sensitive male she has been longing for who listens to her pain and values her as a person and not only as a woman."[8] While the "primarily healthy" woman does not intend to become sexually involved with her pastor, the intimacy that develops in such a relationship "can become sexualized to the eventual regret of both."[9]

"Victims and survivors of incest and sexual assault" comprise Muse's second category. Because these women have repressed their trauma in order to survive, their capacity to identify and assertively draw personal boundaries is badly impaired, especially in the dimension of love and sexuality. When a woman in this situation comes in contact with a pastor who is susceptible to sexual misconduct the consequences are predictable.

The third type of vulnerable woman appears more sinister, for she is plagued with what Muse calls "borderline personality organization." Such women tend to be immensely dependent, possessed by great fear of abandonment and lacking in "impulse control." Because they have not integrated the opposite dimensions of their own emotional life, they "quickly idealize the persons to whom they are attracted, only to devalue them later for what they perceive as rejection."[10] Left unchecked, this tendency leads to what the movie industry has marketed as "fatal attraction." Colleen, the seductive female Bustanoby encountered, may have been struggling with tendencies similar to these.

The final category encompasses codependent, addictive persons, or to follow Muse's characterization, "women who love too much." They lack a healthy self-image, because as children they never received the love they needed to affirm themselves. As a result, such women are attracted to men whom they and others perceive as powerful. Because they are constantly seeking approval from these men, they are too willing to oblige them by shaping themselves to fit their expectations. As Muse notes, "They have trouble distinguishing the assertive, healthy, life-giving 'martyrdom' of love from the unconscious life-taking doormat variety."[11]

Muse's attempt to pinpoint the psychological roots of vulnerability reminds us that to blame any of these women for the pastor's sexual failure is simplistic and indefensible. Indeed, no conduct on the part of a congregant can serve as an excuse or rationale for a minister's inappropriate behavior. Regardless of the situation he encounters, the pastor (or therapist) always retains the responsibility to control his personal behavior and focus on the healing of the client. The person who is unable to do so has no business in the ministry. In chapter seven we will set forth the implications of this assertion for the church and its role in dealing with clergy sexual misconduct.

Because the vulnerable woman is always a victim in incidents of clergy sexual misconduct, we cannot simply dismiss her in order to salvage the ministry of the pastor. We must make certain that we minister to her wounds and needs, which the pastor's actions have seriously compounded.

Ensuring Justice Through Due Process

When our highest priority moves away from protecting the good name of the church or salvaging the pastor's ministry, we are free to focus our concern on the victims of the act. Concern for the victimized congregant means that we seek to ensure that she is justly treated. We can act on her behalf in several ways.

Bringing the act to light. First, justice means that there be no cover-up. A never-ending series of political scandals stand as an ongoing reminder of the devastating long-term implications of whitewashing evil. Yet in the church we sometimes think that hiding the truth somehow serves a higher purpose. We erroneously believe that not disclosing the sexual misconduct of church leaders—allowing their misdeeds to go by unnoticed—somehow will serve the cause of the gospel. The Scriptures provides no foundation for such thinking.

The Bible refuses to expunge the errors of its heroes from the history it narrates. Biblical authors recite the transgression of our first parents, Cain's murder of Abel, Noah's drunkenness, Abraham's willingness to allow Sarah to become the wife of a Canaanite king, and David's adultery followed by the calculated murder of an innocent man. God does not sanction any attempt to cover up the sin or sexual misconduct of anyone—not even clergy. This is evident from the account of Eli's sons. The Bible describes them as "wicked men" who "had no regard for the LORD" (1 Samuel 2:12). They were sexual predators, for they "slept with the women who served at the entrance to the Tent of Meeting" (1 Samuel 2:22). Rather than removing them from office, however, Eli mildly rebuked them (1 Samuel 2:22-25). Eli's cover-up of their conduct led to spiritual disaster in Israel and to their premature death.

Not only does cover-up lack biblical support, it is destructive to all persons concerned. A cover-up injures the offending pastor. It suggests to him that he will never be held accountable for his inappropriate behavior. Further, many abusers are repeat offenders, and inaction leaves them free to continue the inappropriate sexual behavior. Thus the architects of the cover-up are unwitting accomplices in the perpetration of injury to additional victims.

Above all, however, a cover-up compounds the injuries suffered by the immediate victim of the act. By refusing to recognize the harm she has endured, it leaves her victimized a second time. Justice demands that the act be brought to light in an appropriate manner.

Listening to the congregant. Refusing to sweep the incident under the carpet because of our concern for justice leads to a second step. We must give a hearing to the woman involved in the misconduct.

Listening to the congregant is imperative in order to combat our tendency to blame the victim or to allow her to assume a level of responsibility which is not hers. When we make assumptions about the incident without hearing from the congregant, we risk making false conclusions about what happened. Without the information she alone can supply we simply cannot discern what actually occurred. In fact, to draw conclusions about responsibility solely on the basis of the pastor's uncorroborated testimony is foolish. If he has already acted with duplicity, he can hardly be viewed as a disinterested, objective witness. He has lost, at least for the moment, the right to be taken at face value. It is likely that the woman's testimony will shed an entirely new light on the situation. She may not turn out to be a seductress after all. Perhaps our fear that this is the case is what prevents her from being heard.

While we need to hear the woman's testimony to ascertain what occurred, we should also listen to her for her own sake. Whether partial collaborator or innocent victim, she needs to experience healing. In the former case, for true healing to occur she must accept whatever responsibility is *genuinely* hers, and this requires that she be heard. In the latter case, telling her story will not ensure healing, but it can set the process in motion, for compassionate listening soothes the wounds.

Our participation as compassionate listeners, however, requires that we overcome our tendency to avoid painful encounters. As Marie Fortune declares,

> *Compassion* is the willingness to "suffer with" another person coupled with the desire to alleviate the suffering. Often in our own discomfort at another's circumstances, we try to minimize, explain away, or avoid her suffering. We may tell ourselves that it is out of our concern for her pain that we do these things but, in fact, it comes from our discomfort. We simply want to avoid sharing another's suffering. We wish the problem would go away. Compassion is the willingness to be present, acknowledging and listening, even when we cannot solve the problem.[12]

The church seems ready to listen sympathetically to a fallen pastor; the time has come to direct a compassionate ear to his victims as well.

This suggests that the other woman must also be heard for the church's sake. Failure to hear her places the church on the side of the powerful, rather than the powerless. It means that the congregation will inevitably side with injustice rather than justice. And it will lead the church to ignore the needs of the most vulnerable in order to protect the perpetrator. Indeed, without acknowledging the violation, without protecting the vulnerable from further abuse and without calling all persons to accountability, the church cannot claim to be acting in accordance with our Lord's model or in keeping with his mandate for his followers.

Launching an accountability process. Third, justice requires that the congregation put a formal accountability process into operation immediately. In chapter seven we will discuss this process from the perspective of the church. Here we merely indicate its importance in the quest for justice and for the sake of the well-being of the victimized woman.

From the perspective of this woman, the goal of an inquiry is not to resolve a conflict between two parties but to advocate for those who have been harmed and to call the offending party to account. Therefore, when it becomes apparent that sexual abuse has occurred, we must set aside for a time the desire to absolve the pastor or even to salvage his ministry. Instead we must direct our attention and energy to the task of promoting justice.

Justice in the wake of sexual misconduct may include removing the offending pastor from office so that he is no longer in a position to victimize others. Fortune offers the chilling reason this is crucial: "When a minister like Donovan behaves unethically and the authorities merely express concern and issues a warning, he is likely to be more discreet in the future but not likely to change his behavior."[13]

A credible process must treat the incident both as a sexual sin and as a breach of professional ethics. In the past, conservative churches have tended to focus solely on the *sexual* aspect. As a consequence, the central goals of their formal processes tended to be gaining forgiveness of the sin involved, facilitating reconciliation with the offending pastor's spouse (if he was married) and salvaging his ministry. Unfortunately this approach ignores the victim (who has generally been viewed as at least a cooperating sinner or at worst as the perpetrator of the situation that led to the downfall of the pastor).

Mainline churches, in contrast, often overlook the sexual aspect and describe the misconduct solely as a breach of *professional* ethics. This approach falsely separates the professional and personal dimensions of life, and it draws a sharp distinction between *personal* and *professional* ethics. Ultimately this tactic implies that premarital or extramarital sex constitutes misconduct only when it occurs with a congregant or in some other aspect of his professional role.

Assisting the Woman as a Victim of Sexual Violence

Central to our ministry to the "other woman" is the desire for justice. But it cannot end there; it must include standing by her in the healing process.

Healing is never attained quickly. As Willard Gaylin notes, "Time does not heal all wounds, and the amount of time needed to heal the majority of serious wounds is well beyond that which the unwounded could ever anticipate."[14] Victims of sexual violence face an especially difficult struggle.[15]

The greatest service we can offer the congregant in the healing process is to help her come to grips intellectually and emotionally with the trauma of what has happened to her. We must assist her in seeing the clergy misconduct as an abuse of power as well. This means walking with her, as in her attempt to make sense out of the experience she struggles with the unanswerable question, Why? This entails acting as a sounding board as she seeks to deal with her sense of guilt and shame, which arises from the sexual dimension of the act. And if she is to move toward healing, we cannot be shocked or forsake her when she reveals a deep anger not only against the perpetrator, but also against herself and against God. Through it all, we must listen patiently, show Christlike compassion and repeatedly encourage and reassure her.

The congregant attains an important milestone in the healing process when she is able to forgive the offender. Too often we want victims to move to forgiveness as quickly as possible. True forgiveness takes time. As David Stoop and James Masteller remind us, "When you forgive too quickly, without adequately working through what has happened and how you feel about it, your forgiveness is incomplete."[16]

Consequently, the victim must address the matter of forgiving the perpetrator only in conjunction with other issues. Stoop and Masteller outline six steps in the process of forgiveness[17]:

1. Recognize the injury.
2. Identify the emotions involved.
3. Express your hurt and anger.
4. Set boundaries to protect yourself.
5. Cancel the debt.
6. Consider the possibility of reconciliation.

A victim of clergy sexual misconduct will find the difficult road to true forgiveness easier to travel if she is accompanied by wise caregivers who are aware of the enormity of the task involved.

Finally, the healing process includes being able to reaffirm her identity. The congregant who is led across the forbidden zone likely came to her pastor in order to heal her bruised sense of self. Instead of obtaining what she sought, however, she emerged from the relationship more wounded than before. To minister to her in this situation means helping her refocus her fragile sense of identity toward the only source of genuine personhood—the loving God who in Christ declares her to be his beloved daughter.

Because an act of sexual misconduct affects the "other woman" who is often marginalized in the situation, ministry to the victims must address her needs. Equally often overlooked are the other family members affected by the deed, including the pastor's spouse and children, as well as the family of the "other woman." They suffer different, but real, effects of his actions.

Ministry to the victims, therefore, means giving attention to them. It includes such difficult matters as helping them move from bitterness to forgiveness and assisting them as they seek to overcome the resultant dislocation in their lives. But foundational to all such ministry is the realization that they too are victims of the act of indiscretion.

Helping the Pastor's Wife Pick Up the Pieces

The family member most directly affected by the discovery of clergy sexual misconduct is the pastor's wife. Whereas the difficulties his children suffer will be long-term and may not even surface until a later time, the minister's marriage partner faces an immediate crisis. For her, the sexual infidelity of her husband likely means total devastation. For this reason, we must focus our care resources on the pastor's spouse as early as possible, at least as soon as the illicit relationship becomes public.

Ministry to the spouse must begin with our own attitude toward her. Only then will we be able to assist her in working through the grave questions she faces.

Seeing the wife as victim, not perpetrator. Many people assume that if the minister has an affair, the fault is not his but rests with the women in his life. If the "other woman" is not a seductress, then his wife must be a failure. Because we perceive that a good marriage is the best defense against sexual misconduct, we tend to trace the responsibility for an indiscretion to an inadequate marriage. Lying behind this assumption is the unbiblical supposition that it is the wife's job to keep her husband happy. Thus if he is not happy—and the affair would seem to prove this—the wife is to blame for his adultery.

To minister adequately to the wife, we must combat this erroneous assumption. The success of a married pastor is partially dependent on maintaining a good marriage. However, we dare not use the erroneous converse to shift the blame for an affair from the pastor to his spouse, thereby minimizing his responsibility. Marriage is never uniformly satisfactory. No marriage is without its down times. If these periods give license for an adulterous affair, almost every marriage partner could claim a rationale for infidelity at some point. The truth is, the pastor who falls into sexual failure is often the kind of person who enters marriage with unreasonable expectations. Blaming the marriage and the spouse only legitimizes his unrealistic and self-centered expectations rather than confronting, challenging and changing them.

To minister to the wife, we must also realize the difficulties she faces as a pastor's wife. Pastors' marriages have not escaped the trauma of modern marital breakdown. Most people do not sufficiently recognize the extent to which pastors' wives are under stress.

Roy M. Oswald, who conducts burnout workshops, reports that clergy wives score at least as high on stress tests as their husbands.[18] Oswald cites a number of causes, including the current ambiguity over role expectations: "Clergy wives may be clear about who they are, but they continually encounter parishioners who have other attitudes and ideas about how they should talk, dress and engage in congregational activities."[19] To compound the difficulty, clergy wives lack pastoral care. Oswald claims that no one can be both spouse and pastor to the same person. Who, then, is *her* pastor?[20] Also contributing to her stress is the repeated change in geographical location required of her as a pastor's wife. Relocation means coping with the children's resettlement; the loss of her support group and, in some cases, of her professional status; and the difficulty of finding a new support system. All of this takes time. Money is a perennial pressure in most pastors' homes, and the wife too often bears the day-to-day stresses that accompany the management of a limited budget.

In their book *American Couples*, Philip Blumstein and Pepper Schwartz highlight the destructive consequences of the intrusion of work into a marriage: "People's jobs are commonly seen as competing with time and energy that could be spent on the relationship and so they are very often a source of conflict."[21] The pastoral vocation dominates every aspect of the marriage, and in many ways the pastor's wife bears the brunt of its impact. Blumstein and Schwartz note one potential problem: "A husband may feel he suffers enough stress from his own work and therefore it is unfair of his wife to burden him with hers."[22] In short, the pastor's wife may live in a situation in which his vocation dominates and hers is excluded. If she is at home with small children her concerns can easily be trivialized.

Unless the couple understand this dynamic and take resolute steps to balance their relationship, disaster awaits them. Quality time spent together—sharing personal joys, frustrations and anger—goes a long way in recovering the toll extracted by pastoral ministry.

David and Vera Mace report that half of all clergy couples are "dissatisfied with their attempts to communicate effectively, to manage their negative feelings and to resolve their conflicts successfully."[23] They are especially concerned about anger, which they find to be a common emotional problem in clergy marriages.[24] Public suppression of anger coupled with dumping it on the marriage partner creates emotional and spiritual damage that can devastate any marriage. But it is a particular hazard in a clergy marriage and particularly dangerous for the pastor's wife.

Even in the best of circumstances, the pastor's wife carries heavy emotional and spiritual burdens, often without the resources that are usually available to other church members. As the Maces conclude, "We get a rather disturbing picture of the clergy wife carrying a heavy load. Denied adequate time for maintaining the intimate relationship with her husband, she often feels lonely and frustrated."[25] In many ways she can become an emotionally abandoned person.

When her husband is moving to the brink of the forbidden zone, the difficulties the pastor's wife faces compound. Whether the minister acknowledges it or not, certain women in the church will find him attractive. When this happens he will discover how easy it is to accept their uncritical admiration as a welcome contrast to his wife's more realistic view of him. In response, his affection and intimacy with his spouse may wane at precisely the time when she needs greater reassurance of his love and understanding. Finally, as he crosses the forbidden zone, her sense of self-worth wilts.

Once her husband's illicit relationship becomes publicly known, her situation deteriorates even further. She suffers the humiliation of public scandal, and she finds herself carrying the blame that insensitive congregants readily place on her shoulders. Her struggle is exacerbated by an inquiry which generally ignores her and readily dismisses her needs as irrelevant.

Heather Bryce writes from her own experience about the trauma faced by the wife of an unfaithful pastor. She reports about losing her self-worth not only because of her husband's adultery but also because she was now denied involvement in the ministries where she received approval.[26] Bryce also describes her sense of isolation; most difficult of all was the realization that if she were able to stay within the marriage relationship, her only companion would be the man who hurt her.[27] Bryce justifiably complains that everybody else was able to go on with their lives—everyone except her. She acknowledges the resources she found in her relationship with Christ. But she poignantly observes that whatever support they received as a family from Christ's church was directed to the assumed needs of her husband—their pastor. Throughout the narrative, Bryce refuses to paint her husband in a negative, destructive light. It is surely not unreasonable to expect that the church would do the same for her and others who share her plight.

Insofar as both partners are sinful and therefore contribute something to marital failure when it occurs, the wife of a pastor who strays does carry some responsibility. But we dare not point the finger directly at her and use her assumed faults as a rationale for supporting the offender and ignoring one of the prime victims. The time has come for the church to take care of the female victims of clergy sexual misconduct and not simply work at rehabilitating the offender. Could it be that our focus on the pastor is yet another tragic illustration of the gender blindness of so many church people?

Helping her sort through her questions. Once his action is known, the pastor's wife faces the difficult task of accepting the reality of what has happened. Even though she did not will it, her world has changed, and it will never return to its former state. Like the other woman, in this new situation the pastor's wife faces a host of grave questions which she must face squarely if healing is to occur. Like that of the victimized congregant, her road to healing will be easier to travel if wise and compassionate facilitators walk with her. Ministry to the pastor's wife, therefore, includes standing by her as she seeks to handle the questions whirling through her mind: What role did I play in his act? Under what circumstances can my marriage be salvaged, or will the situation lead to divorce? How can I get on with life, given the fissure his act has caused?

Her first response is likely to seek to affix blame. Initially, she may defend her husband. To do so, she may blame the other woman (because she apparently seduced him), the church people (because of the stresses they imposed on her husband) or perhaps herself (because she failed as a wife). While all of these persons may have contributed to what happened, the primary responsibility for the sexual misconduct properly belongs to her husband. She needs to believe this. To do so, she may need caring people to assist her.

At the same time, if she and her husband were experiencing marital difficulties, the pastor's wife needs to reflect honestly on her role in the marriage. She must accept whatever responsibility is rightly hers, while not exonerating her husband for his action. To walk this delicate pathway, she will need caring people who can help her separate the truth from what may be a strong tendency on her part to deal too harshly with herself.

In many ways sexual misconduct is similar to a death in the family. Healing requires that the pastor's wife acknowledge, rather than deny, her pain and grief.

The acknowledgment of grief includes adding up her losses. Even though these will be different for different women depending on their emotional and spiritual background, in every case the losses are severe. As Heather Bryce's experience indicates, these losses include the destruction of her feeling of self-worth, forfeiture of the ministries in which she was involved, a gnawing sense of isolation that accompanies the withdrawal of her support structures, and the shock that paralyzes her into inactivity and prevents her from getting on with her life. In a sense she is experiencing a trauma worse than the death of her husband. Had he died, she would have been the recipient of an outpouring of support; but the disgrace she faces inflates her needs while deflating the level of support others offer her.

Losses such as these can take a heavy toll. They may produce anger and depression, which are not necessarily inappropriate reactions. Healing requires that the pastor's wife acknowledge these emotions and not allow their presence to add to her sense of guilt. This process is expedited by the help of caring people who are willing to walk with the pastor's wife through the emotional quagmire.

Finding appropriate caregivers may not be easy. Sometimes the right people simply emerge. But in the majority of situations the pastor's wife will need to take the initiative, as unfair and difficult as that is. She must seek out a support group who will walk with her, providing both encouragement and accountability as her delicate self begins to mend.

As if these losses were not sufficient, the pastor's wife must cope with the added burden posed by the discovery that duplicity and deceit lay at the heart of their marital relationship. This may cause her to doubt her capacity for making sound judgments. She may wonder: How did I come to marry a man like this? How could I not sense what was going on? Such questions raise doubts about her ability to make appropriate decisions about her future: Can we deal with this and keep our marriage intact? Do I even want to keep the marriage together?

Many variables will be at work in determining whether or not the marriage survives. If the pastor's wife determines that her husband is a predator, restoring the relationship becomes a monumental task. If the sexual indiscretion was an atypical act of a wanderer, the prospects for renewing the relationship are brighter. If he sincerely repents and genuinely accepts responsibility for the behavior, they may find in Christ the spiritual resources that enable them to engage in the rebuilding process. For rebuilding to occur, however, counseling may be necessary. Were the congregation to provide the financial resources for this, it would not only be a gracious gesture but also a clear example of the church functioning as *the church.*

Should the pastor's wife and her repentant husband stay together, theirs will be a different marriage, of course, but not necessarily an unsatisfactory one.

The most difficult task the pastor's wife faces is that of putting her husband's sexual misconduct behind her and moving into the future—whatever future she chooses. Most people who face a traumatic experience eventually get on with their life. So will the pastor's wife. Yet her new life will be different from the way things were. Above all, she will likely never be as trusting as she once was. This change may loom as the most difficult issue she must confront in the long term, and confronting it will require all the resources she can muster. Unless the process of healing allows her to overcome the gnawing distrust the act of sexual misconduct embedded in her psyche, her wounded spirit could in the end destroy her.

Ministering to the Pastor's Children

An illicit affair creates grave difficulties for the pastor's wife. For his children, however, it produces long-term devastation. Unfortunately their needs are often completely overlooked in the process of rehabilitation. Only in rare cases do they receive any assistance in working through their pain. They are more likely to become the forgotten people, as the congregation focuses its attention on the pastor and the attempts at damage control.

When they hear of their father's action, the pastor's children sense a deep humiliation. As the affair becomes public knowledge, they are aware of the whispers and hear the gossip that follows them wherever they are. They may face public humiliation as well.

Public humiliation sometimes surfaces in a tragic manner. The church may require that the pastor confess his failure at a public meeting. This may prove to be a horrible experience for the children, particularly if they are present. To witness their father suddenly being transformed from a much loved and admired pastor to a public pariah can leave emotional scars that may never heal. Several years after it occurred a pastor's daughter still speaks about the terrible Sunday on which her father was required to make a public confession at the morning worship service. "I felt my life collapsing," she recalls.[28] The incident resulted in the breakup of her family, leaving her and her sister wards of the state.

If their parents' marriage does not survive the crisis, the pastor's children will suffer all the repercussions of divorce. But in addition to the loss of a stable family environment inflicted on all children of divorcing parents, they will lose their place within the congregation. Even if they are eventually able to settle in a new fellowship, the knowledge of their fallen father may pursue the family, causing a continuing sense of public humiliation and ostracism.

Clergy sexual misconduct brings long-term effects on the psychological and spiritual development of the children. One potentially affected area is sexual development. A child's dawning awareness of and attitude toward sexuality is, in large part, dependent on what he or she observes in the home. Their father's unfaithfulness and the difficulties it poses for their parent's marriage—whether it remains intact or ends in divorce—jeopardizes the ability of the fallen pastor's children to develop a healthy view of sexuality.

Linked with that potential, their father's unfaithfulness and the public trauma that ensues may destroy the children's ability to trust. The destruction of trust poses grave difficulties for their future abilities in matter of commitment, conflict resolution and intimacy. But even more tragic is their possible disillusionment with the very spiritual resources to which they would normally turn for counsel and comfort—their parents, especially their pastor-father, and the church. Years after witnessing her father's public confession, the pastor's daughter still remains disillusioned about their former congregation: "I'm mad. They could have handled that situation totally differently. I have no desire to go back. . . . I don't understand where they're coming from at all."[29]

Comforting the Family of the Abused Woman

The fallout from clergy sexual failure is extensive. The ripples radiating from this stone thrown into the pool of life never seem to end. Entire family systems can be affected. The effects on the pastor's family can be drastic. But the ripples may engulf other family members as well, the family of the victimized woman.

These people are likely to be affected indirectly, as they suffer the repercussions the traumatic experience works on this woman. Clergy sexual misconduct lowers its victim's sense of personal worth and robs her of her innocence and spontaneity. As a consequence, the victim's ability to establish or maintain healthy sexual relationships is impaired. This victimization, in turn, affects others.

The indirect victims may include the woman's children, if she is a mother. They may face many of the difficulties encountered by the pastor's children—humiliation, destruction of trust, loss of primary sexual role models. Whereas the pastor and his wife may stay together, the abused woman's marriage is less likely to weather the crisis, for it probably was shaky before the sexual misconduct occurred. For these children, therefore, the trauma of a separation looms on the immediate horizon.

Another indirect victim may be the present (or future) marital partner of the affected woman; he must cope with the fallout from the illicit relationship. One spouse offers this assessment of the situation: "Too often the church is a perfect place for abusive men. They can parade in sheep's clothing until in the intimacy of the counseling office, or when they have arrived to comfort a troubled parishioner, they undress and show their fangs and claws."[30]

The spouse confronts problems greater than merely his wife's distrust of the pastor and the church. She may inadvertently view him as if he were that pastor. The husband of the abused congregant explains: "Occasionally an unexpected move, a misplaced comment, causes a flicker of distrust to register in the corner of her eye and the ghost of another man passes over our bed and leaves us both chilled."[31] A courageous and committed couple can work through these residual problems and eventually enjoy an even deeper bond with each other. But for every couple that overcomes an adversity like clergy sexual misconduct, there are many others for whom the residue is simply too debilitating.

We can understand, therefore, that the husband of a woman who was sexually violated by her pastor writes passionately about it: "Does the church you attend or are thinking of attending have a policy of specific action to deal with sexual offenders? If not, stay at home. The male dominated church leadership has not taken this issue seriously enough. You and your children would be better, physically and spiritually, humming your favorite hymn in the mall on Sunday morning."[32]

The immensity of the wounds an incident of clergy sexual misconduct inflicts on its many victims obligates the church to live up to its calling to be caring disciples of Christ, who in the name of their Lord reach out to hurting people with God's own compassion. True ministry to the victims—the abused woman, the pastor's wife and the family members involved—will be challenging, exhausting and probably even expensive. But ultimately it is unavoidable, and its rewards are great. The potential benefit such ministry offers is glorious. Perhaps as the church comes to be perceived as acting in this caring, redemptive manner it will regain the respect it has lost through the epidemic of clergy sexual misconduct and gain a hearing for the gospel it cherishes. As this occurs, the Holy Spirit will lead many to join in the praise to the God who brings light out of darkness, even out of the darkness of clergy sexual failure and the wounds it inflicts.

For this to happen, however, the church must think through and put into place a properly informed, healing plan for responding to the problem. Before exploring this topic in chapter seven, we must focus on the pastor himself and what he can do to keep from succumbing to the lure of sexual misconduct.

6
The Pastor
& the Prevention
of Misconduct

C lergy sexual misconduct has become a debilitating epidemic in our day. For the church, its apparently meteoric rise raises profound questions about what we teach and practice concerning two central aspects of human existence—sexuality and power. Bound up with these issues are the practical questions about prevention: How can we stem the tide? How do we respond constructively to the phenomenon?

Some voices offer a straightforward solution to the problem: the church should simply weed out those who are likely to engage in an onerous act before they are placed in leadership. This suggestion has some obvious merit. The old adage that the best predictor of future behavior is past behavior has considerable validity. Churches ought to take seriously their divinely given role in ordaining only persons of spiritual maturity and moral integrity. The New Testament emphasizes godly character, pure conduct and impeccable reputation as necessary qualifications for pastoral leadership (1 Timothy 3:1-13).

At the same time, the complexity of the phenomenon precludes any easy answer. There is presently no sure-fire way of predetermining exactly who will fall into sexual sin. Even past behavior, which often provides an indication of future risks, can never speak the last word, because the gospel can transform the life of a past offender. According to Jack Balswick and John Thoburn, "No one factor in and of itself can be identified as the reason why a given minister succumbs to a sexual temptation. In most cases a combination of factors contributes to their behavior."[1] Consequently, John Theis's assessment is correct: "Some form of pre-screening or testing for the likelihood of being a sexual abuser is not easy, indeed is probably not possible at the present time."[2]

Another factor precludes screening as an easy solution to the problem of clergy sexual misconduct. If propensity of falling into sin were sufficient to bar a person from church leadership, who would be worthy of ordination? Indeed, a good leader is not a person who never senses the pull of temptation, but rather one whose commitment to Christ and reliance on the Spirit's power leads him or her to live a consistently moral life.

These considerations indicate that the best initial step in launching an offense against clergy sexual misconduct is to equip pastors (and future pastors) in prevention. Central to this equipping task is pinpointing those factors which facilitate us in withstanding sexual temptation.

The considerations set forth in earlier chapters suggest that pastors who never compromise their sacred trust are guided by a personal commitment to biblical standards of morality together with a deep sense of vocation. In this chapter we focus on additional, and perhaps more tangible, characteristics that foster moral behavior and so enhance a pastor's ability to avoid sexual misconduct. Pastors who withstand sexual temptation are characterized by a deep sense of personal susceptibility which, coupled with an understanding of the dynamics of the clergy role, forms an "antenna" alerting him to potentially dangerous situations. Crucial as well are the support systems a pastor develops—those persons who hold him accountable to biblical standards of behavior and to the vocation to which he has been called.

Our ability to live in accordance with biblical morality and to avoid illicit sexual activity is enhanced by self-awareness—a deep consciousness of who we are. This self-awareness includes a sense of personal identity derived from a vital relationship to God in Christ. For the pastor, self-awareness also entails a keen sense of vocation derived from a divine call to the ministry.

To these positive aspects of self-awareness we must add a negative dimension, which is our concern here. No one—not even a dedicated servant of God—is automatically exempt from the pull of the thought of an illicit sexual encounter. Therefore, the pastor who would guard his moral integrity must come to grips with his susceptibility, both as a male pastor and as an individual.

Awareness of Susceptibility as a Male Pastor

Many pastors too readily assume that their position as church leaders somehow exempts them from the lure of sexual immorality. Even the most godly pastor, however, is not immune to temptation. Each minister is a potential offender. All are capable of yielding to a momentary impulse or of harboring a secret desire and eventually acting on it. For this reason the Bible cautions against complacency and the lack of vigilance. The Preacher warns, "Pride goes before destruction, a haughty spirit before a fall" (Proverbs 16:18). And Paul adds, "If you think you are standing firm, be careful that you don't fall!" (1 Corinthians 10:12).

Susceptibility to sexual sin begins, of course, with attraction. Because we are sexual beings, we are naturally sexually drawn to many persons. Being a pastor does not elevate a person beyond such feelings. On the contrary, most pastors will find themselves from time to time sexually attracted to a congregant. Left unchecked, sexual feelings can precipitate a powerful temptation to express that attraction through some overt sexual act. So the pastor who would minister with moral integrity must confront at the onset any sexual feelings he develops for a congregant. Such confrontation begins with self-awareness. The pastor must be cognizant of his feelings and honestly acknowledge the sexual attraction that he senses.

Pastors are susceptible to sexual temptation because they—like all humans—are sexual beings. In addition, however, their role as professional caregivers marks them as special targets for sexual failure. The tendency shared by males in our society to want to "fix" everything is especially evident among clergy. This mystique can be devastating. It may render a pastor unwilling to admit that his personal skills have limits. Nor might he always be able to recognize when a counseling situation actually lies beyond his expertise. When this subtle pride combines with sexual attraction, the pastor is a candidate for the trap of maintaining the counseling relationship long after he has ceased providing positive spiritual care to the congregant.

The male mystique coupled with the pastoral office may lead a minister to become a rescuer. The rescuer goes beyond appropriate willingness to help and assumes full responsibility for providing the solution to the sensed needs of another. Quite aside from any susceptibility to sexual temptation it may introduce, playing the role of rescuer is emotionally and spiritually exhausting. It is also unfair to the congregant because it robs her of the opportunity to learn how to deal with life's difficulties, and how else can she find personal growth and an increased sense of self-worth? Being a rescuer creates a co-dependent relationship that is counterproductive for all persons involved.

Rescuer-pastors are susceptible to sexual failure because they too easily see themselves solely as healers and never as persons who also are in need of healing. The dynamic of a hurting male pastor, on a crusade to fix every problem and heal every wounded soul, offering care to a broken and wounded female congregant can be dynamite. Teresa Tribe and Douglas Wilson capsulize the danger: "A male pastor placed in such a situation with a distressed female parishioner may experience a strong temptation to personalize the relationship. He may find himself crossing over healthy boundaries and fulfilling his own personal needs by imagining that he alone is the one who can rescue this woman."[3]

Awareness of Personal Susceptibility
This scenario leads us to the other, more personal aspect of our susceptibility,

our individual woundedness. The pastor who would serve with moral integrity must not only realize that he is prone to sexual temptation as a male member of the clergy. He must also become aware of the dimensions of his own life which contribute to his susceptibility. He must become cognizant of his own vulnerability.

Many personal factors could make a pastor a candidate for sexual failure. At the heart of his susceptibility, however, are the pastor's own deep-seated insecurities, which readily emerge in the dual dynamic of unacknowledged sexual and power needs. As his low self-esteem produces a sense of power-lessness, a pastor may attempt to bolster his self-esteem through the perversion of power he hopes to find in an illicit sexual liaison. The debilitating demands of the ministry and his need for affirmation—sometimes compounded by difficulties in his marriage—may combine to set him up for sexual failure, for which his caregiving relationship with a congregant provides occasion.

Vulnerability may be fueled as well by the pastor's unresolved questions about his own sexuality. Traditional pastoral training customarily warns future male clergy about the so-called seductive woman. Unfortunately, such ministers are seldom adequately equipped to affirm their sexuality as an essential dimension of their being that God declared "good," while acknowledging its grave destructive potential. As a result, a pastor often moves through his career burdened with baggage that he has never properly processed. These unresolved personal issues readily surface in the caregiving role, especially in counseling relationships.

Much of the destructive baggage we carry through life stems from past experiences that have left lasting scars. Some may date back to childhood or adolescence, comprising wounds that have festered beneath the surface of our consciousness for years. We go through life as wounded persons, and this woundedness contributes to our being vulnerable in the face of sexual temptation.

Ordination does not automatically bring wholeness in our lives. Church leaders, like other people, often carry deep wounds from their past. The pastor who would guard his moral integrity acknowledges his own wounded-ness and hence his vulnerability. He realizes that the lure of forbidden sex may actually be a symptom of his search for healing for his own wounded sense of self.[4] Aware of this aspect of his life, he then takes appropriate steps toward personal healing.

Personal healing may come in various ways. Recognizing the emotional and spiritual realities of one's own life is a giant step toward healing. But the New Testament nowhere assumes that we are to fight any of these battles alone. Personal healing generally requires the involvement of others. For example, sharing one's own struggles with a counselor who combines spir-itual direction with perceptive emotional insight can be a crucial step in the healing process.

Above all, the pastor who would experience emotional healing must truly desire to have the Holy Spirit create Christlikeness—which Paul describes as "the fruit of the Spirit"—in his own life (Galatians 5:16-25). The apostle reminds us that our ultimate enemies are the powers of darkness. For victory in this spiritual battle we need divine resources which only the Spirit can provide (Romans 7:14—8:17; Ephesians 6:10-18).

Awareness of Addictive Tendencies

For every minister the road to prevention of sexual failure leads through awareness of his susceptibility as a male pastor and an understanding of his vulnerability as an individual with a personal life history. Some pastors, how-ever, will need to travel an additional pathway to moral integrity. For them, the trail includes coming to grips with the possibility that they are caught in sexual addiction.

For the pastor whose sexual behavior is out of control, an entirely different situation has been introduced. Professionally and vocationally he is in an almost irreversible downward slide. To reset his course, he must take imme-diate steps to resolve the sexual issues that have led him into an addictive way of life. He needs to deal with his own feelings of shame, guilt and anger. He must discover what, if anything, of his previous life can be retained, including his marriage and family. Above all, he must be willing to go to appropriate resources for help.

Fortunately help for the addict is becoming increasingly available. Most large communities have sexual-addiction clinics. More and more church groups are offering help. Whichever route the pastor follows, healing will require every resource he can find at a time in his life when so many of his resources are disappearing or forsaking him. The good news is that if a pastor recognizes the abyss into which he is falling and acts before failure stares him in the face, he can find help. The minister who adamantly ignores the danger signals until after he has engaged in blatant sexual misconduct, however, has only compounded his problems and brought grief into the lives of many others.

Prevention of sexual failure requires self-awareness. The pastor who would minister with moral integrity must come to grips with his own susceptibility in its various dimensions. But taken in isolation, this process can end in a cul-de-sac. We often lack the necessary personal resources to deal constructively with the cognition of our own potential for failure. For the pastor this situation is often acute: Where does the minister go with his self-awareness? Who will stand by him, facilitating his journey from awareness of his susceptibility to victory over sexual temptation?

A needed resource lies in the support systems in which the pastor participates. Among the most important of these are marriage, accountability groups and mentors.

Finding Support in Marriage

Many pastors readily acknowledge that the loving relationship they enjoy with their spouse is the single most important factor contributing to the success of their ministry.

A wholesome marriage consistently reinforces sexual fidelity. In the words of Robert J. Carlson, "having a good marriage is a very important factor in maintaining appropriate sexual behavior in one's professional relationships."[5] Carlson's conclusion finds confirmation in the research of Balswick and Thoburn: "Over one fourth of the pastors cite their relationship with their wife as the most important reason for sexual fidelity."[6] At the same time, they note, "Marital dissatisfaction coupled with work boredom is the kind of situation that has been conducive to the most fantasy and openness to actual liaisons."[7]

A good marriage contributes to sexual fidelity by providing a wholesome, God-ordained context for physical sexual expression. But beyond this obvious role, the marriage relationship offers the pastor a foundational, permanent support system. In fact, marriage is the most consistent, long-term source of support many pastors experience.

Marriage functions as a support system as it facilitates honest communication. Indeed, an open relationship with a loving spouse provides a wounded pastor with a sympathetic ear to whom he can voice his experiences of self-discovery. The wise wife will even welcome her husband's acknowledgments of sexual attraction to a congregant, without feeling threatened by them.

In the supportive relationship, listening also evokes response. Crucial in the healing process are verbalized encouragement and admonition.

Support, however, must be seen as a two-way street. We are growing increasingly aware of the heavy emotional and spiritual burden facing today's pastor's wife in even the best of circumstances. A minister's expectations that his wife be understanding and supportive, therefore, must be balanced by his own willingness to understand her burdens, to encourage her to share these and to support her gladly and unreservedly. A commitment to mutuality, as implied in Paul's advice to the Corinthians (1 Corinthians 7:1-5), can produce a strong bond between the pastor and his wife that will see them through whatever difficulties they may encounter.

The supportive role of marriage is not limited to the communication it offers between husband and wife. The marital covenant itself can play a supportive role, as it provides a focus for the pastor's sense of accountability. For the married church leader, obedience to the ordination vow includes fidelity to the marital vow. In a sense, the latter may even symbolize the former. Many pastors testify to occasions in which they gained the victory in the moment of sexual temptation simply by remembering their commitment as a marriage partner.

While acknowledging the importance of a healthy marriage, we ought not to overstate its potential. A mutually satisfying marriage cannot by itself guarantee sexual fidelity. Nor does a commitment to singleness doom a pastor to a perpetual sexual struggle. No one should enter into a marriage solely to gain a support system for the sake of one's ministry.

The focus on marriage also erroneously leads some people to assume the validity of what they see as the converse, namely, that when a pastor falls into sexual sin his wife is to blame. While marital bliss is often a contributing factor to sexual fidelity, we can neither hold the pastor's wife responsible for the pastor's sexual decisions nor excuse the sexual indiscretion of a single pastor because he has no wife to keep his passions in check.

Becoming Accountable

We live in an age of individualism. "You mind your own business, and I'll mind mine," is the dictum of modernity. Unfortunately, the individualism of our age has engulfed the church, as well as society. The cult of "me" is a contributing factor in the epidemic of clergy sexual failure. If rampant individualism is among the root causes, accountability relationships offer a crucial antidote. Our Lord himself underscored that his disciples need to hold each other accountable. Likewise, pastors who would minister with moral integrity do well to foster relationships with people who will offer lines of accountability.[8]

In addition to marriage, the lines of accountability a pastor establishes may take many forms. When a minister senses he is susceptible to being drawn into sexual temptation arising out of a specific situation, he ought to consider forming an ad hoc support system, consisting of one or more clergy peers or congregational leaders. The primary purpose of the group is to encourage the pastor who requested its support, while holding him accountable through the duration of the situation. For example, a pastor might discover that he (or she) is developing a sexual interest in a counseling client. The support group can stand with him until he is able to place the congregant under the care of another. Such groups provide what Tribe and Wilson call "a model of collegiality in which we can ask for and receive confidential support from peers when involved in highly charged pastoral relationships."[9]

While ad hoc support systems provide accountability in difficult situations, they cannot replace participation in an ongoing accountability group consisting of clergy peers or lay church leaders. Don Basham issues this poignant call: "Any minister who has not found and submitted himself to some form of personal oversight, which can provide not only encouragement but also correction, is in danger of rebellion and deception."[10]

Ad hoc groups focus on the specific difficulty faced by one member. Long-term accountability clusters, in contrast, exist for the benefit of all members. They offer mutual support and provide a context in which pastors can share their ongoing struggles and experience healing from the deep wounds they may be carrying. To provide the kind of ongoing accountability that ministers need, however, the group must hold strictly to a code of confidentiality.

Emulating Role Models and Mentors

Pastors who marry can hope to discover the delight of a permanent support system offered by a good marriage. Both married and single pastors can experience victory and healing through ad hoc and ongoing accountability groups. Not to be overlooked by either, however, is the important supportive contribution that mentors make to successful ministries.

Developing a relationship with an esteemed seasoned pastor is especially important for those who are beginning their ministry. But we never outgrow the need to look to others as models. Being mentored by others includes tapping into their wisdom and advice about situations encountered in the pastorate, including sexual struggles. But a mentor's impact transcends verbal communication. Pastors who have remained faithful in the area of sexuality can provide significant role models to other clergy, holding them accountable to emulate their example as they have emulated Christ's (1 Corinthians 11:1).

One of the discouraging aspects of the present epidemic of clergy sexual failure is the number of mentors who have violated their sacred trust. The list of renowned leaders who have fallen is heartbreaking for all Christians. But especially affected are those pastors for whom they served as mentors or who looked to them as role models. Their failure does not mean that we should avoid or abandon all mentor relationships. The pain inflicted when human mentors demonstrate that their feet are made of clay provides a poignant reminder that we dare look to the "heroes of the faith" only in order to be directed through them to the Source of our faith.

The highest focus of accountability for each believer is Christ. Our Lord is the greatest role model and mentor for his disciples. Pastors who would live in sexual integrity as Jesus did can glean valuable insight from Jesus' manner of ministry, including his way of relating to women.

The Gospels do not present Jesus as a man who avoided women lest he fall prey to sexual temptation. On the contrary, our Lord freely associated with them. In fact, he contravened social mores by engaging women—even women of questionable reputation—in intimate conversation. Regardless of the sexual history of the women he encountered, Jesus ministered to them without moral compromise. How was our Lord able to avoid sexual failure? How was he able to maintain his integrity and the integrity of others?

Crucial to Jesus' success in ministering to women with integrity was his profound self-awareness. J. Steven Muse offers this insight: "Presumably Jesus felt free to be intimate with women without fear of misappropriating the relationship for sexual and romantic ends because he was *intimately acquainted with the source of his own motivations* (John 2:25)."[11] His sense of identity grew out of his knowledge of himself as a man accountable to God. Jesus was motivated by his desire to glorify his Father by fulfilling the vocation God had entrusted to him. Our Lord viewed each woman he encountered (and all persons) through God's eyes. Rather than seeing them as objects for his personal gratification or as means to his own ends, he viewed each as a person with spiritual longings, deep-seated aspirations and grave needs.

Motivated by his sense of mission in each situation, our Lord directed whatever erotic feelings a woman may have felt for him to the deeper longing of her heart. As Muse notes, "In his intimate encounters with women, he was able to lead each one to a recognition of her intimacy with the God for whom she truly yearned and whom she sought to glimpse and touch through him."[12]

As Christ's disciples, male pastors are called to minister to women in the same way he did. And his model of ministry provides the ultimate accountability structure for clergy in their commitment to fulfill their vocation with moral integrity.

Prevention of clergy sexual failure requires that a pastor (or future pastor) become conscious of his own susceptibility to temptation. This self-awareness should evoke from him the desire to communicate openly with those who form his support systems, in order that he might remain accountable at all times and move toward personal healing. But what about the actual contexts in which he is called to minister? What considerations will assist the pastor in responding with moral integrity in the crucible of ministry?

Perhaps no aspect provides a more powerful context for sexual temptation than the pastor's role as a caregiver, especially in counseling situations. The pastors who would consistently minister with moral integrity, therefore, must pay attention to the dynamics of pastoral care.

Balancing Closeness and Distance in Pastoral Care

Attention to the dynamics of pastoral care begins with a proper understanding of the purpose of the caregiving relationship. The pastor who would minister with integrity must know what he is attempting to accomplish in this aspect of his involvement.

The ultimate goal of all pastoral care is to enhance the well-being of the congregant.[13] Counseling promotes well-being in that it contributes to the counselee's sense of independence and the development of an authentic personal identity. Toward this end, a counselor assists people in sorting out both their inner drives and the external influences on their lives, so that they are empowered to cope with the situations they face and to act with integrity.

To be effective, pastoral care requires that the minister become sufficiently close to the counselee so as to perceive the wounds and hurts that lurk beneath the surface. This closeness can open the door to improper intimacy and possible sexual involvement. Distance provides a measure of protection for both the congregant and the pastor from the forces that threaten the integrity of their relationship.

The danger that intimacy introduces into the relationship requires that pastors balance closeness with detachment. The pastoral care role challenges the minister to ascertain what constitutes the proper balance between the two and to maintain that balance when faced with the tug toward improper intimacy. Muse capsulizes the minister's dilemma: "How do we protect the pastoral relationship from romantic and sexual contamination without sacrificing the heart-to-heart relationship with Christ's people which is the wellspring of true ministry?"[14]

Maintaining proper distance is not merely a check on inappropriate intimacy. It is crucial to effective counseling. Rather than being antithetical to compassionate closeness, distance provides the space in which true, healthy compassion can emerge. Whenever a counselor becomes too emotionally involved with a counselee, the bond endangers the minister's objective perception of the counselee's situation. Unless a healthy distance is maintained, therefore, compassion may become corrupted. For this reason Walter Wiest and Elwyn Smith conclude, "A mature professional possesses the ability to project concern that unites compassion with appropriate distance."[15]

But whose responsibility is it to make sure that closeness is safeguarded by the proper distance? Because of their wounded condition and client status in the relationship, counselees are often unaware of the importance of maintaining distance. Nor can they always perceive when the boundary of proper intimacy has been violated. The role of the counselor, in contrast, requires a far greater degree of objectivity and a commitment to preserve the balance needed to facilitate the goal of the counseling situation. Similarly, in any caregiving relationship the pastor must take the responsibility of establishing an appropriate and safe distance, not only to avoid crossing the boundary into improper intimacy but also to insure the effectiveness of the caregiving ministry.

Understanding Sexual Attraction

The dynamics of the caregiver role demand that a pastor understand the importance of a healthy balance between closeness and distance. At no time is maintaining appropriate distance more crucial than in situations in which the congregant evidences a sexual attraction for the pastor. This is the point in the counseling relationship at which sexual exploitation is most likely to occur.[16] The pastor's response will largely determine whether the relationship becomes a source of healing or degenerates into an exploitative and abusive situation which can only exacerbate the congregant's woundedness.

Consequently, the pastor who would minister with moral integrity and foster healing in the life of the congregant under his care must understand the deeper forces at work when a counselee's erotic feelings are awakened.[17] We cite several aspects of this dynamic.

It is not unusual for a wounded congregant to develop feelings for her pastoral caregiver. J. Andrew Cole points out the forces at work in all such counselor-counselee relationships: "Erotic feelings can easily arise in a therapeutic relationship, where two people meet alone and discuss the most intimate details of life. The patient may view the clinician as the most kindhearted, stable, wise, reasonable and calming presence he or she has ever met. Naturally, under these circumstances, the clinician becomes important to the patient and erotic experiences can unavoidably become a part of the situation."[18]

What the pastor perceives to be awakened sexual feelings on the part of the congregant, however, may be an expression of deeper longings and needs. Pamuela Cooper-White offers this warning: "If a parishioner acts out sexually, the minister should recognize it as a clear cry for help. The *last* thing he should do is read it as a valid invitation."[19] Rather than enhancing the pastor-congregant relationship, for him to allow her sexual feelings to occasion his sexual advance could jeopardize any healing that his ministry might otherwise have brought about in her life.

The reason is simple. Thirty to seventy percent of women who seek psychological treatment report a history of sexual abuse.[20] The woman with whom a pastor senses an erotic relationship emerging and with whom he is tempted to have a sexual relationship may be like "Kathi Carino." As a child she was deeply wounded by a father who took her into the basement "where he stripped me naked and whipped me with his belt before raping me" and who "dressed me like a saloon girl at age ten and took pictures of me while a young man 'made love' to me."[21] The wounds that scarred Kathi's young life left her with both a deep distrust of people and a need for acceptance. She writes, "If I could have a nickel for each time I have asked my therapist if he hated me or each time I asked him to promise not to leave me, I would be a wealthy woman."[22] Were her pastor to interpret her attraction to him as the license for a sexual indiscretion, his act would be yet one more step in the downward spiral destroying her sense of person. It would be another stark reminder that men in authority are not trustworthy.

Knowing the Warning Signs

The vulnerability of the counseling process has lead some to conclude that either pastors should not counsel at all or that male pastors should restrict their counseling to male congregants (and leave the counseling of females to other females). This latter solution is advanced by conservative thinkers, who are generally motivated by the desire to protect the male pastor from the seductive woman. Recently, however, feminists have joined the chorus. Maxine Glaz, for example, calls for a "reevaluation of the male psychological norms of most pastoral training."[23] While she does not explicitly declare that men should not counsel women, the degree of understanding of the female psyche Glaz finds essential effectually eliminates men from this role.

The fact is, however, that the vast majority of male pastors simply cannot restrict their counseling in the manner critics advocate. They cannot avoid counseling female congregants if for no other reason than because of the minister's role as crisis counselor. When a person dies the pastor is inevitably involved in grief counseling, however brief it may be. When there are serious marital or family problems, the pastor is often the person to whom the individual or family members—including the women involved—will turn. Even if the male pastor speedily refers a female congregant to another caregiver, he has initiated a counseling relationship.

Counseling across gender lines is an inevitable part of the pastor's vocation. Therefore, the solution to the problem of susceptibility is not to wish the pastoral role were other than it is, but to take the necessary precautions to preclude falling prey to sexual temptation. This may include working with the congregation in setting up guidelines for a minister's counseling work. A recent Southern Baptist study suggests the following conditions for pastors doing counseling:

1. Always have another person in the church building when counseling a woman.

2. Install a door on the counseling office which prevents total privacy (such as a door with a glass insert).

3. Publish counseling guidelines, including counseling hours and days, with an acknowledgment of the extent and limits of individual training in counseling.

4. Create a referral list which is considered "safe," and actively make referrals to these professional therapists.

5. Decide in advance how much touching is appropriate and, if so desired, state in writing that hugging, holding hands, etc., is inappropriate.

6. Ask the church to pay for the services of a mental health professional as a supervisor/consultant in counseling matters, and establish regular times to consult with this mental health professional.[24]

Although such guidelines may be helpful, precaution means knowing and always being alert for the signs that the relationship is approaching the forbidden zone. A pastor may enter a counseling relationship fully intending to maintain a proper balance between closeness and distance and fully cognizant that a congregant's expressions of apparent sexual interest in him mask deeper needs. Yet as his relationship with a woman under his care progresses, he may begin to develop sexual feelings for her while remaining unwilling to admit the danger that these feelings pose for both of them.

Violation of the boundary of proper intimacy rarely occurs imperceptibly, however. Generally it is preceded by ample warning signs.[25] Six such warning signs are especially significant[26]:

1. The conversation he shares with the congregant is becoming increasingly personal, as the pastor talks unduly about himself or shares a similar experience to that of the congregant.

2. The pastor's physical contact with the congregant has moved beyond a warm handshake to friendly pats, perhaps even hugs.

3. The pastor finds himself fantasizing about a sexual relationship with the congregant and does not dismiss such thoughts.

4. The pastor offers to drive the congregant home.

5. The pastor begins to arrange meetings with the congregant outside of his normal, established counseling routine (such as over lunch or in conjunction with other events).

6. The pastor discovers that he is increasingly desirous to hide his growing feelings for, interest in, and meetings with a congregant from his accountability systems, especially his spouse.

Actually, anything that blurs the distinction between therapy and the rest of life or between the roles of caregiver and friend is a warning signal. When a pastor perceives that he is beginning to blur these roles—even in his mind, let alone in overt action—the time has come for him to take stock of his ability to continue to provide pastoral care to the congregant. Because he can easily be caught by a propensity to refuse to acknowledge a growing sexual interest in a counselee, the married pastor should entrust to his wife the right to veto a long-term counseling relationship with any female congregant.

Reducing Personal Focus

In all caregiving relationships, pastors and congregants meet on unequal footing. The dynamic involved powerfully affects both participants in the relationship. Especially problematic are the sexual feelings that can be awakened in the congregant and the pattern of countertransference into which the minister may fall. So a pastor must take steps to reduce the likelihood of arousing undue sexual feelings in congregants as he ministers within the context of the pastoral calling.

The danger of improper sexual feelings which besets the pastor-congregant relationship is exacerbated by traditional church structures which emphasize the central role of clergy in congregational life and ministry. As we noted in chapter four, the pastor often unwittingly becomes the focus of the erotic feelings of congregants. Although the negative effects of such structures can never be eradicated, they can be reduced.

To this end, pastors must encourage a healthier (and more biblical) understanding of the ordained role, namely, that of facilitator of the shared ministry. In this model, the minister's primary function is to lead the congregation in engaging in the mandate that all share, including that of providing "pastoral" care and counseling to hurting people. When the ordained minister no longer forms the focus of attention, he is less likely to become the central object in the erotic dynamic of the pastoral care role.

The Positive Potential

For some male pastors, the risks involved in ministry to women may simply be too great. A male minister may find that he is not able to function as caregiver when the possibility exists that the woman in his care may become sexually attracted to him. Perhaps he is struggling with his own sexual identity. Maybe he is involved in pornography or some other addictive behavior. Or he may easily fall into sexual fantasy while possessing a great capacity to rationalize his unwholesome behavior. Whatever the debilitating problem, for him to engage in counseling women would pose a serious professional and personal hazard. Nor can he actually function effectively as pastor to the congregant under such circumstances.

For pastors who do not struggle with, or have gained the ability to cope with, these problems, a congregant's sexual interest need not merely occasion danger for their integrity in ministry. It can also interject a moment of opportunity for true inner healing. As Peter Rutter so poignantly declares, "Every forbidden-zone relationship in which sexual tension appears also presents an opportunity to heal."[27] J. Andrew Cole explains the psychological dynamic that can allow for such healing: "It is, in fact, the spontaneous awakening of real feelings and attitudes (including erotic ones) in a sufficiently controlled and structured setting which provides a way to understand and work through them."[28]

The male pastor holds the power to move the arousal of sexual feelings beyond mere personal temptation into an opportunity for healing of deep wounds. He alone can turn an impending sexual disaster into a life-giving moment. To do so, he must deny his instinctive tendency to take the congregant's expression of erotic feelings at face value and—to use Rutter's words—"give up his sexual agenda toward her, once and for all."[29]

Once this occurs the pastor can work with the congregant in identifying the anger, depression and loss that these feelings often obscure. Together they can explore the painful memories, unhealthy patterns of relating to males, and other harsh realities that the congregant may have developed throughout her life but which are now masquerading as presumed love toward the pastor. As Cole notes, "By substituting professional objectives with romantic ones, the problems which made treatment necessary in the first place are avoided."[30]

The lure of illicit sex is not to be minimized. Living in a society that focuses on sexual encounters and minimizes the biblical ideals of fidelity in marriage and abstinence in singleness, even ordained ministers are not immune from the powerful pull and the danger posed by sexual temptation. Pastoral care situations often offer the occasion for clergy sexual failure. But no pastor need succumb. Through proper prevention—self-awareness, the development of support systems and understanding the pastoral care dynamic—not only can male pastors minister with integrity to women under their care, but they can also turn the moment of temptation into an occasion of healing for their congregants as well as themselves.

Despite our best attempts at prevention, however, clergy sexual misconduct does occur. What steps should the church take in such situations? In our final chapter we turn to this question.

7
The Church's Response to Misconduct

T he Reverend Dr. Charles Smith, a gifted orator with a large international following, had enjoyed a highly successful ten-year ministry at First Church before returning to his home country to accept a prestigious denominational position. Three years after his departure the church council of his former congregation arranged to have him serve as guest preacher during the anticipated six-week absence of their current pastor. First Church considered itself fortunate to have an ongoing connection with a person of Dr. Smith's stature.

When Mary Jones heard the news of Dr. Smith's imminent return, she became distraught. In a tearful visit to James Harvey, a clinical psychologist and member of First Church, she described the sexual harassment to which Dr. Smith had repeatedly subjected her while acting as her pastor. Harvey went straight to George Jackson, who chaired the church board. To his dismay, however, Harvey found Jackson totally uninterested in discussing the matter, even though Jackson himself acknowledged receiving a written complaint of sexual misconduct from another female congregant. Jackson informed Harvey that the situation demanded a simple response. In strictest confidence he would instruct the leading church deacon to warn Dr. Smith to watch his conduct during his ministry at First Church.

Each incident of clergy sexual misconduct leaves a host of victims in its wake—the abused woman, the families of the two parties, other congregants. But beyond those immediately involved, the epidemic is adversely affecting the church of Jesus Christ, defaming the reputation of its Lord and undercutting its message. Because the perpetrators come from the leadership ranks—those who are called to embody its ideals—clergy sexual misconduct is ultimately a problem for the whole church. The church must take the lead in dealing with this debilitating phenomenon.

But what exactly is the church's role in responding to clergy sexual misconduct? What responsibility must the church shoulder in such cases? How we answer this question determines to some degree how the church should handle specific allegations of misconduct.

The Church in Denial

All too often when a case of sexual misconduct surfaces within the church, the congregation quickly divests itself of responsibility. Members seek to pin the blame on someone—the victimized woman, the pastor's wife or the pastor himself. Rarely will a congregation consider its own role in the difficult situation.

Marie Fortune suggests that this response is not limited to the church, but is typical of human institutions in general: "Institutions . . . share a pattern of response to the misconduct of an authorized representative and to the public disclosure of that misconduct. An institution acts first on what it perceives to be its self-interest. Seldom does it identify its self-interest to be the same as the interests of the people it is supposed to serve."[1]

The situation Fortune describes certainly corresponds to what transpired in "Peter Donovan's" congregation.[2] When Donovan's victims approached the church president, he indicated that he was responsive to their accusations.

They left the encounter sensing that he was genuinely concerned,[3] and believing that they had found an open, listening ear. However, after seven months of inactivity in the matter, the women received a letter saying that the church leadership would not deal with the issue, except for the reprimand they had administered to the pastor. In an attempt to close the door on any possible confrontation, the president wrote, "There is no question in my mind that the church would be seriously damaged."[4] Nearly two and a half years after the original complaint, the leadership finally took meaningful action. But even then they gave little thought to the victims and absolutely no thought to the "absurd" idea that the congregation itself might bear some responsibility for the situation.

Cases such as this cause us to wonder, What aspects of the life and functioning of the church allow this scenario to occur? It seems that the problem of clergy sexual misconduct is only exacerbated in the context of a congregation that habitually denies its own complicity in the negative situations that arise within its ranks. The current epidemic demands that churches learn to accept proper responsibility for the actions of their leaders.

The Church as a Family System and a Total Institution

Christians readily speak about the church as a family. We heartily sing, "I'm so glad I'm a part of the family of God." Indeed, our shared allegiance to Christ as God's children means that we are a spiritual family. In addition to this foundational theological relationship, as an institution the church often functions sociologically and psychologically in a manner that resembles human families. For this reason several contemporary thinkers appeal to current family-systems theory to understand the dynamics of the local congregation.

Family-systems theory helps explain why clergy sexual misconduct occurs and why an occurrence often precipitates an internal crisis. The family model helps us understand the situation of the ordained leader within the congregational setting.

Often a pastor begins his ministry oblivious to the dynamics of the pastor-church relationship. Uppermost in his mind is his desire to please the church.

But he is woefully lacking in self-awareness and in awareness of how people in his congregation relate to each other and to him as their pastor. In trying to please others he fails to see the various unhealthy ways in which the congregation functions. He allows congregants to invade his personal boundaries, he ignores his own legitimate needs, and he accepts the unreasonable demands of neurotic individuals in the fellowship. In so doing, he settles for enmeshed relationships that are unproductive for everyone. In this manner, a dysfunctional church comes to be led by an increasingly dysfunctional pastor, who is emotionally depleted and therefore vulnerable.

Donald Capps augments this family-systems approach with insight from Goffman's concept of "total institutions."[5] A "total institution" is one which so completely absorbs its participant that they have little or no life outside it. Because institutional life is so all-absorbing, little space remains for freedom of consent.[6] Institutional people simply obey or live out the goals and programs of the institution.

For the pastor, the congregation functions not only as a family system but also as a total institution. This is evidenced by the typical clergy lament, "I have no life outside the parish."[7]

Viewing the church as a total institution helps us see why the pastor who transgresses the "forbidden zone" will likely do so with a congregant. In Capps's words, "The parish is the pastor's world, and parishioners are, in that sense, the only ones who are truly available to the pastor."[8] At the same time, viewing the church as a total institution reminds us why this crime is so heinous. The pastor's participation in a total institution places grave boundaries on his conduct. We may liken the minister's relations with congregants to the relations of staff workers to patients in a long-term hospital or to inmates in a prison. Total institutions such as these can fulfill their mission only when there is a strong taboo against fraternization between staff and patient (or prisoner). Any violations of the boundaries between them carries the potential of hurting both.[9] So also in the church a careful line must be drawn between pastor and congregant for the sake of the well-being of both. The dynamic of the total institution exacerbates the evil inflicted by a sexual relationship involving a pastor and a congregant.

By creating an unhealthy climate for their pastor, the church makes him vulnerable to sexual misconduct. Our intent in viewing the church as a total institution is not to excuse a pastor's inappropriate behavior, to absolve the guilty party or to overlook the question of who the true victims are. Rather, this approach helps us see the wider picture of responsibility. This wider responsibility for clergy sexual misconduct rests on the social system itself. The system includes the congregation that readily becomes a total institution to its pastor, and denominations that continue to support the "total institution" model of Christian ministry.[10]

The concept of "total institutions" indicates how a congregation might share in the responsibility for clergy sexual misconduct. It reminds us that a congregation can and often does consume the life of the pastor. In so doing, the church unconsciously creates the kind of climate in which he becomes emotionally susceptible to sexual transgression. A local church becomes a total institution when it encourages the pastor in his own tendency toward workaholism, nourishes his propensity to allow the "ministry" to take over his whole life, and ignores the fact that in being a "good" pastor to them he is neglecting his marriage and family.

In the eyes of the church leadership, Pastor Robert was a wonderful minister. He never took a regular day off, he was always available on call, and he would drop a family activity at a moment's notice to respond to a parishioner's demand, even if it could have waited till later.

But good Pastor Robert was also continually exhausted and emotionally frazzled. Increasingly he built intimate relationships with people outside his marriage and family. When he eventually crossed a sexual boundary, the church never saw itself as having any responsibility for his failure.

Family-systems theory and the idea of the church as a total institution help us realize that the problems of clergy sexual misconduct run deeper than the personal needs and insecurities of the pastor himself. Clergy sexual failure occurs in the context of a larger family—the church—whose dysfunctional dimensions contribute to the problem. Thus the congregation must accept appropriate responsibility for any incident of clergy sexual misconduct.

In placing blame for sexual misconduct, the church reacts as a familial body. In addition to forming the context for their pastor's indiscretion, the church often functions as a family system in the way it responds to the disclosure of his action. During an internal crisis of this magnitude, many types of alliances—and "misalliances"—readily emerge.

When a congregant accused Pastor Stephen of fondling her breasts, it created a major scandal in the congregation. During the ensuing meeting with the church board, he did not deny the accusation. Pointing out that the woman had a very doubtful sexual reputation, he claimed that she had placed him in a situation where he had touched her only to escape her advances. Because the board was already polarized by many issues that had nothing to do with this matter, this influenced their view; some of the board members believed him, and some did not. Stephen's guilt or innocence quickly became lost in the power struggle that ensued.

More important for our discussion is the typical reluctance—or inability—for a church to focus on itself. Like most families facing difficulties, congregations often find it easier to act as blamers. If the pastor, his spouse, "the seductive female," Satan or even society in general is at fault, the members can excuse themselves from all responsibility. Any suggestion that they are not merely dealing with "a problem child" in their midst but with themselves as "a problem family" lies beyond the comprehension of most local churches. Unable to face their own dysfunctional corporate life, they tend to expel "the problem child," who thereby serves as a scapegoat.

One likely candidate for the role of scapegoat is the minister. As Capps notes, the offending minister is the "perfect scapegoat, because . . . the pastor is important enough to the community that his sacrifice will be considered socially therapeutic, and yet, like the orphan (a common scapegoat) he is marginal enough to the community . . . that few, at least among the congregation's powerful constituencies, will mourn his loss."[11] Alternately, the church may view the expelled pastor as both the offender and the hero who sacrifices himself for the good of the family.

These dynamics indicate that the phenomenon of clergy sexual misconduct involves more than the actual behavior of offending pastors. If this is the case, then its solution must not only focus on pastors but must entail an examination of the church itself as an institution.

Marie Fortune's account of how Newberg Church handled the Donovan affair forms an illuminating example. Their response resembles a family counseling session in which the participants assign blame everywhere except to the family unit itself. Their pastor was an expert at blaming others, but in a sense he merely mirrored the style of the church.

In addition, the congregation had great difficulty acknowledging and resolving conflict. The church leaders did not want to hear from the victims; nor did they want to confront the pastor. Their only concern was to protect the institution. Lying behind their response was a deeper problem, an inability among the leaders to deal with each other directly. Rather than solving the difficulty, they chose not to confront the situation in its stark reality and left the congregation with a dangerous accumulation of unresolved anger.

How should a congregation respond to a situation of clergy sexual misconduct? The necessary first step is acceptance of responsibility. This acceptance includes taking ownership for the pastor's actions. The church called him, and the church must hold him accountable.

At the same time, the church must accept responsibility for its own complicity in the act. The spiritual family cannot merely blame the "identified patient" as the sole cause of its troubles. It must look deeply into its own internal life and assess how it functions as a corporate people (for example, 1 Corinthians 5:1-13).

Let's look at this more closely.

Three Actions Toward Taking Responsibility

Some churches will understandably resent any suggestion that they need to accept some responsibility for the pastor's failure. Perhaps this reticence is due to a too-narrow conception of the responsibility involved. Actually, their responsibility may be varied. As we noted, they may have reinforced the pastor's own compulsive behavior which contributed to his failure. They may have failed to set in place an adequate policy on sexual behavior. Or perhaps they failed to follow through with the process outlined in the policy. In addition, the congregation may have been so wracked with conflict that it simply wore out its pastoral leadership. Or it may have sacrificed the pastor and his well-being, allowed him to become the scapegoat, rather than deal with its own internal conflicts.

The relationship of pastor and church is unique. A congregation rarely asks its pastor for detailed information about how he spends his time. We can understand that to do so risks turning the ministry into an eight-to-five job. But we must not minimize the cost involved in leaving the pastor on his own. It often means that neither lines of healthy accountability nor structures of genuine support become part of the pastor-congregation relationship.

A wise congregation hears an accusation of sexual misconduct against the pastor as a wake-up call. It is an alarm, admonishing the church to look carefully at its own internal dynamics as well as its relationship to its pastoral leadership. In short, the congregation must accept responsibility for what has transpired and what may still be happening in the pastor's life as well as within the ongoing dynamics of church life.

The church can take three actions toward acknowledging responsibility for their pastor's misconduct.

The first action: Every congregation or church body must carefully devise policies that address the various issues involved in this phenomenon. Such policies should both govern the behavior of its leaders and form a point of reference in the event that allegations of sexual misconduct emerge at any time.

The second action: The church must act immediately when it receives a credible complaint of clergy sexual misconduct. To facilitate a fair hearing, the complainant ought to recount the incident in the presence of members of both sexes. We will look more closely at the process of hearing and pursuing a complaint in the next section.

The third action: The responsible church must take seriously any actual case of clergy sexual misconduct. Its membership must refuse to sweep the occurrence under the rug or deny the event's significance for them as a body. Rather than passing off the incident as the result of the individuals' personal problems, the congregation should use the occasion to spark genuine reflection on their internal working as a church family. This intensive soul-searching should lead the congregation to acknowledge whatever blame is rightly theirs and to do whatever they can to aid healing in the lives of all persons touched by the incident, but especially the primary victims.

To take every allegation of clergy sexual misconduct seriously is to follow the demands of the New Testament (1 Timothy 3:1-13; James 3:1; 1 Peter 5:1-4). Even Paul's caution "Do not entertain an accusation against an elder unless it is brought by two or three witnesses" (1 Timothy 5:19) points in this direction. Of course, the intent of the apostle's guideline is to protect an elder from capricious or malicious charges.[12] But we dare not use the text to protect a pastor from a genuine accusation, for after giving this guideline Paul demands that elders guilty of unacceptable behavior be admonished: "Those who sin are to be rebuked publicly, so that the others may take warning" (1 Timothy 5:20). The apostle provides no support for those who would minimize the serious consequences for an errant pastor's attempt to evade credible charges.

Curbing the tide of clergy sexual misconduct requires a broader response on the part of the church than simply taking responsibility. The response must extend to the education of persons training for church leadership. We must design educational experiences that assist future pastors in understanding the intricate dynamics at work when someone violates the "forbidden zone." Education should likewise heighten ministerial students' awareness of their own susceptibility to temptation. And ministry training ought to instill in future leaders wholesome attitudes toward their own sexuality that free them to develop wholesome relationships with the opposite sex.

The role of theological education is not our central concern in this chapter, however. Rather we want to explore the more immediate response of the church to incidences of clergy sexual misconduct, the aim of which ought to be to effect a "zero tolerance policy" toward any such betrayal of trust.

Denominational Structures and the Local Congregation

The church must put in place adequate structures for dealing with allegations of clergy sexual misconduct. Because ordination and the pastoral office are not limited to any local congregation, denominations must take the lead in establishing appropriate structures. Many denominations have already given serious consideration to their responsibility in this matter.[13] Those who fail to do so only imperil themselves and the congregations they serve.

The exact structure a denomination develops will reflect its own governing polity. Yet certain elements should be present in all such structures, regardless of denominational affiliation. For example, every structure must provide a proper mechanism for reporting allegations of misconduct. This includes a means for selecting and appointing a knowledgeable person to whom information concerning alleged abuses can be directed. In addition, each structure must delineate channels though which the victims of misconduct can receive appropriate support. At the heart of all such structures must also be an effective investigation process. This process must expedite the gathering of information, ensure a fair hearing to all concerned persons, and lead to the removal of a proven offender from office for the sake of the abused and the protection of potential victims.

Beyond these immediate steps, the structure a denomination devises must facilitate certain long-term objectives. These include the rehabilitation of the offender as a believer—that is, his restoration to a proper relationship to God, to the victims and to the church. When this goal is accomplished (and only then), the structure must provide a means of discussing the question of the former pastor's possible reinstatement as a church leader.

Unfortunately, a wide gap exists between what denominations inaugurate and what local churches implement. Many of those touched by clergy sexual abuse bitterly point out the inexcusable discrepancy between what denomination study papers so nicely advise and what their local churches actually implement (or fail to implement). This apparent lack of integrity often leads women, who are by far the majority of victims, to sense that the church has betrayed them.

To bridge this gap, each local church ought to have a written declaration of how it will handle allegations of sexual failure. Depending on the polity it follows, the process may simply place the congregation within the structure its denomination has established, or it may delineate a thorough procedure that the congregation itself will oversee. When the denomination is the main adjudicating body, it must inform the congregation whose pastor is the alleged offender which process is being used. Otherwise the gap between the denominational procedure and the perceptions within the local church will break down at both ends.

Clergy Sexual Misconduct and Interpersonal Disputes

But how should the church—whether in its local or its denominational expression—proceed? Some Christians would argue that Jesus himself provides detailed instructions that apply to every interpersonal dispute in the church, including clergy sexual misconduct (Matthew 18:15-20). Following the pattern our Lord outlines, they reason, the first step in dealing with an accusation of sexual misconduct requires a face-to-face encounter between the accuser and the alleged offender.

At first glance this suggestion seems both reasonable and biblical. But on closer inspection the difficulties inherent in this interpretation emerge. The text suggests that the situations Jesus addresses are largely private, personal matters. He instructs us in what we should do when we feel personally wronged by another believer. Clergy sexual misconduct, however, is never merely a private matter, even though it includes a personal dimension. Our discussion in chapter three indicates that the sexual nature of the alleged offense and the involvement of a church leader mean that each allegation is always a church concern.

Further, in the text, our Lord seems to be addressing persons who share a peer relationship: "If your brother . . ." (Matthew 18:15). His advice describes how two believers should sort out a situation that threatens their relationship. The process he sets forth assumes equality, perhaps even gender equality. As we noted in chapter four, however, equality is absent in cases of clergy sexual misconduct. Such situations usually involve a vulnerable woman—a congregant—who has been violated by a powerful man—her pastor.

This leads to an additional, related difference which places allegations of clergy sexual misconduct outside the realm our Lord addresses. If the accusation is true—if her pastor has indeed led a congregant across the forbidden zone—she may be emotionally unable to confront him. (Our discussions in previous chapters suggest that were the victim capable of standing up to her pastor, the incident may not have happened in the first place.) Or for various reasons, including shame, guilt, denial or fear, a victim may be reticent to confront her pastor.[14]

Finally, requiring that a congregant confront her victimizer privately as the first step can actually work against Jesus' desire that victims receive justice. The offending pastor can all too readily use such confrontation to silence his victim and even persuade her that she is responsible for what happened. So a confrontation may result in the perpetrator continuing the offense and even widening the scope of his victims.

If the pastor could not silence her, he still would likely protest her accusations. Nor can she expect a sympathetic reception from whomever she subsequently approaches with the problem.

The likely scenario is confirmed by Nancy R. Heisey's findings.[15] She reports that each of the women she surveyed who attempted to confront the offender were met with strong denials. Many who then solicited help from other church members or leaders found them reticent to believe their story and unwilling to act. When other people did give the women a hearing, the victims suffered intense pressure to bypass the biblical injunction mandating public confrontation ("tell it to the church") for the kind of generous forgiveness Jesus enjoins on Peter in the next incident in the text (Matthew 18:21-22). Heisey observes: "The call to forgive often replaces a clear call to bring the matter to the community when the offender has not repented and offered restitution privately."[16] The rush to dispense with justice in the name of forgiveness offers a simple solution to which many churches gravitate when faced with "messy" situations.

A Procedure for Governing Cases of Sexual Misconduct

These difficulties lead us to conclude that our Lord does not intend that the process given in Matthew's Gospel govern cases of clergy sexual misconduct. Because of the dynamic of the alleged offense, we cannot place on the congregant the difficult and often debilitating task of confronting her pastor in private, followed by an attempt to seek out sympathetic members of the congregation who might assist her. Rather, the church must use a procedure that can place all concerned parties in a position to be heard, defended and justly treated.

The adjudication of an allegation of clergy sexual misconduct must move deliberately and methodically, following several well-defined steps.

Step 1: Hearing the Informal Accusation

A congregant will probably find the thought of voicing a complaint against her pastor traumatic.[17] She is often a vulnerable person who fears rejection. She finds herself torn between guilt and shame. She feels a mixture of anger and confusion. And she anticipates being met with denial, disbelief and alienation. For these reasons the church must put in place a process that signals to congregants its commitment to responding quickly, justly and compassionately to every credible accusation.

Whether or not the church appoints a specific person to hear all such complaints, the congregant may initially voice her story to someone whom she both trusts and sees as being in a position to act on the disclosure. Whether or not the person who receives the information believes it to be true, he or she has a moral obligation to demonstrate pastoral concern to the distressed congregant. If for some reason the confidant will not be involved in processing the charge, he or she must inform the congregant, indicating to whom the complaint will be referred, and undertake to contact the appropriate person as soon as possible. Because of the nature of the charge, delay is not acceptable, for it may endanger not only the congregant but other potential or actual victims.

At this point, the person who will lead in the ensuing process should contact the congregant. They should arrange for an immediate face-to-face meeting involving congregational representatives of both sexes. (The involvement of both men and women at every stage in the process is crucial.)

During this initial meeting a complex set of dynamics will no doubt be operative. The complainant will constantly assess how the others are receiving her. She may be trustful or suspicious, depending on her past experiences, her relationship with the church and her appraisal of the attitudes of the people at the meeting. Her own emotional makeup, her sense of self-worth and security, and her spiritual state will contribute to her demeanor. At this stage, however, her chief concerns are simple: Am I being heard? Do they believe me? Do they blame me? Will they side with their pastor?

The interviewers may well be in a state of shock. Their love and respect for the pastor or their desire to avoid a scandal may tempt them to seize any opportunity "to shoot the messenger." They will be frantically assessing both the complaint and the complainant: Could the allegation be true? Can we believe this person? Is she emotionally stable? Does she have a problem with her own sexuality?

Little wonder all participants are anxious!

The listeners must assess not only the veracity but also the seriousness of the alleged offense. The narrative they hear could include any number of charges: verbal or nonverbal sexual harassment, accidental or deliberate sexual violation, genital sexual activity with or without actual penetration and with or without either apparent consent or real consent. (Or the alleged offense could involve many other behaviors which are not the focus of our discussion, including voyeurism, child molestation or homosexual activity.)

Once her story is heard the complainant is entitled to an explanation of the process that will ensue. At this point, she must decide whether or not to proceed. In some situations, it may be essential for the church to investigate the case, even if the complainant decides not to press the allegation. If she decides to move to the more formal hearing that follows, she must commit her charges to writing and outline them in a clear, specific and reasonably documented manner. Clarity in this document will ensure that those involved in the formal hearing are absolutely certain of the exact allegation they are considering. A written allegation also ensures that the accused pastor knows exactly what he is alleged to have done.

Finally, the interviewers ought to compose a written summary of the preliminary meeting. The complainant should have access to this document and be given opportunity to respond to it orally and, if necessary, in writing. These actions must transpire in a loving, caring context that presumes neither the guilt nor innocence of the alleged offender and avoids all prejudicial assumptions about the complainant.

All parties must maintain strict confidentiality until the completion of the next stage in the process—the preliminary conversation with the alleged offender. Without breaking confidentiality or divulging in any way the nature of the situation, those directly involved should solicit prayer from persons they deem spiritual, concerned members of the congregation. A sad commentary on the state of the North American church is that fervent prayer rarely, if ever, is included as a crucial part of the process of dealing with any difficulty it faces.

The focus of prayer must not be limited to the anonymous petitions for pastor and congregant. The committee involved in the proceedings needs God's guidance, strength and protection. However these people handle what follows, some members of the congregation will become emotionally upset and direct their anger against the committee participants personally.

Step 2: Confronting the Accused Pastor

A meeting between the pastor and the interviewers should follow as soon as possible. The same people who heard the complaint (a committee consisting of both men and women) should both initiate and conduct the session. They should schedule the meetings to ensure that confidentiality will not be breached.

Before meeting with the pastor, the committee members must prepare themselves for the session. They must be thoroughly acquainted with the factual details of the complainant's story. But they must also prepare themselves spiritually and emotionally for what will transpire. Theirs will be no easy task. They will need divine resources to act fairly, firmly and pastorally.

As in the initial meeting with the complainant, a complex set of dynamics will operate during the confrontation. The pastor's response may include disbelief, indignation, anger, evasion, denial, anxiety, panic, shame and perhaps confession. The function of the committee is not to make an accusation but to explore an allegation that another has made. Their ability to keep this role in view will depend on the seriousness of the allegation, the nature of their relationship to the pastor, the health of the church and their own emotional and spiritual makeup. Even in the best of situations this meeting will not be pleasant for anyone. It will be riddled with anxiety, emotional tension and perhaps intense spiritual conflict.

Just as the complainant is entitled to loving, compassionate concern, so is the accused. Nevertheless, the committee members must be realistic in their expectations of the outcome of their caregiving. Regardless of his guilt or innocence, the pastor will be hurt. Their relationships will never be the same again.

The chief purpose of the meeting is to communicate to the pastor the allegation of sexual misconduct. Our legal tradition dictates that the committee members maintain the presumption of innocence, but they dare not cavalierly dismiss the allegation. Regardless of their personal feelings, they downplay the seriousness of even the most improbable accusation only to the peril of the church. Even if we believe that in these situations the pendulum has swung too far in favor of the complainant, we must acknowledge that our context has changed—and for understandable and legitimate reasons.

What response can the committee expect from the accused pastor?

If the minister is a sexual predator, he may use all the means in his power to deflect or deny the charges and to intimidate, delay and even harass those who dare to question his integrity. He may welcome the confrontation as a means to halt any further proceedings.

Marie Fortune's account of Peter Donovan's actions when confronted suggests what the committee can anticipate in similar cases. Donovan strategized how best to use his wide support within the congregation to thwart any action that might be taken against him. He went so far as to threaten to pull the church out of the denomination, believing he had sufficient support from the membership to effect this move.[18] In the end, he did not have the votes needed to accomplish his goal. But his aborted attempt indicates that Donovan was prepared to destroy anything and anyone who threatened his position and status.

Fortune describes such a person as "manipulative, coercive, controlling and sometimes violent."[19] The committee needs to know that such a person will use every trick in the book—and many that are not—to maintain control. Regardless of the means he uses, the committee cannot allow the predator to succeed in derailing the process.

The wanderer, in contrast, may immediately admit the truth of the accusation, especially if he has been struggling with his conscience or is aware of the serious consequences of his actions. His confession, however, places the committee in an awkward position. All those present at the confrontation will be justifiably relieved by this acknowledgment. Yet in the exhilaration of the moment, they may end the proceedings on the spot. To do so, however, is to fail to do justice or correctly handle mercy.

When confronted with an accusation of sexual misconduct, Pastor Jonathan, who had been carrying a load of guilt and shame, immediately pleaded guilty and wrote a letter of resignation to the congregation he was serving. The deacons, wanting to avoid divulging the details to the church and hence to preclude the scandal that would ensue, latched on to the resignation as a quick, clean solution to what they thought could develop into a messy situation.

Jonathan, however, was a popular person in the congregation. When the reason for his hasty departure became known, those who had been touched by his ministry were irate. In their minds, he was the victim. They blamed the "other woman," the deacons and others in the congregation whom they now believed had been out to get the pastor. In the emotional intensity of the moment, they voiced scathing allegations, and their subsequent actions nearly split the church.

Pastor Jonathan did not fare well either. Though he had served the church for a number of years, he now found himself not only without a job but also without any severance arrangements. Because he had voluntarily resigned, he was ineligible for either denominational or government assistance. But financial stability was not his chief loss. Jonathan's family life was in disarray. His sense of self-worth eroded. And his support system evaporated. Later he deeply regretted the spontaneous resignation that had left him abandoned, nearly destitute and on the verge of suicide.

What the committee had deemed a quick and painless solution turned out to be neither. Apart from opening the way for the disaster that followed, their ready acceptance of their pastor's resignation cut short a process which is intended not merely to remove an offender from leadership, but to expedite healing in the lives of all persons involved in or affected by the sexual indiscretion. Jonathan's sense of abandonment on the heels of their short-sighted response led him to focus on his own hurt and the grievance against the church that lodged in his heart. This focus allowed him to avoid dealing with the issues surrounding his inappropriate behavior.

Besides intimidation or confession, the committee can anticipate a third possible response. The pastor may contest the allegation of sexual impropriety. He may meet the charge with vehement denial—even moral indignation. Or he may put a spin on it so that the alleged incident no longer appears serious.

Whatever the response of the pastor, the committee must conclude the confrontation by outlining the process that will follow. Unless special circumstances require the involvement of the civil justice system, the procedure is best kept within the jurisdiction of the congregation or denomination. The adjudicating body must be careful to follow due process in accordance with the church's code of ethics (whether written or merely assumed) and its method of dealing with disciplinary matters. Any failure of the congregation or denomination to be consistent with these could encourage the pastor to file a civil suit and possibly trigger a court judgment overturning their verdict and awarding him damages, even if the pastor is guilty of violating church standards. If the church has no code of ethics and no set process in place, the committee should seek to gain the agreement of all parties, if possible, to an ad hoc procedure that will govern the situation.

As with the initial meeting with the complainant, the committee must compose a written summary of what transpired at the confrontation. They should focus on factual information, not impressions or conjectures, and outline the steps that will follow. The pastor must receive the same opportunity to respond to this statement as the complainant had to the summary of her meeting with the committee.

Both summaries form the core of what the committee now reports to the denominational leadership, the governing body of the congregation, or the church itself, depending on the operative polity and the position held by the accused. Regardless of polity, however, sometime after the two preliminary interviews the congregation must be informed. The attempt to retain confidentiality beyond this point can only be counterproductive. The news will spread too quickly!

Step 3: Holding the Formal Hearing

After the committee selected to investigate the charges has made a preliminary report on the meetings with both the accuser and the accused, the more formal process commences. Churches following congregational polity will likely call a meeting of the membership at this point. Doing so moves the entire process into the public arena. Unless the matter is handled with great discretion it has the potential to split the church.

Because a formal hearing cannot occur immediately, the church must determine the status of the accused pastor during the interim period. A potentially credible accusation of sexual misconduct is a serious charge. By raising questions about the pastor's integrity, it automatically calls his ministerial position into question. Formulating a response that is both sensitive to the one bringing the accusation and fair to the accused will require a high level of discernment on the part of the church leadership. The tendency in the past to brush aside such accusations will tempt some churches to overreact and others to do as little as possible.

If the accusation comes from someone who is perceived to be a responsible person and if it is of such gravity that if proven it will result in the dismissal of the pastor and/or his loss of ordination, the church has little option other than to release the pastor from his duties for a period of time.

Suspension will be painful for the pastor. He may fear that this act will damage him both personally and professionally. He may view it as a violation of the legal principle "innocent until proven guilty." However, in situations where a public trust is at stake, suspension is the best alternative. For example, a police officer who faces a serious charge of professional misconduct is either suspended (with or without pay) or transferred to a post that does not entail contact with the public. In any case, all parties must keep in mind that suspension is not a declaration of guilt. It just seems the best way of ensuring that justice is done.

The details of the suspension, such as its length and financial implications, may depend on the seriousness of the charge, the credibility of the complainant and the size of the church.

By the time of the formal hearing the members of the congregation may have overcome the initial shock and disbelief that likely characterized their reaction to the news of the accusation. If polity dictates that the local church pursue its own inquiry, great care must accompany the selection of the review panel. The congregation may be so polarized that even the appointment of people to the inquiry sparks a bitter, contentious debate.

To ensure that the committee has access to competent advice, the congregation should consider engaging a consultant to assist in the process. This person should have a professional background in sexual issues and should be familiar with the life of the church. The accused pastor and the complainant should each nominate someone to serve on the panel, thereby ensuring that their case receives fair treatment. The church should round out the panel with additional members who can both assist in reaching a fair verdict and provide equal gender representation. Likely candidates for this panel are the persons who conducted the original interviews with the complainant and the pastor.

In most situations the inquiry panel should engage in its work without the presence of legal representatives of either the complainant or the accused. However, the church may need to confirm with a legal specialist that they are indeed entitled to proceed in this manner in their locale.

The panel of inquiry must decide with the parties involved whether their sessions will be open to the public. The pastor may be the most likely person to object to an open hearing. Yet in most situations if he is innocent he has little to lose and much to gain. And an open hearing may placate the complainant's concern that her accusation be taken seriously and dealt with expeditiously.

The church may prefer public access because it allows the members to assess the fairness of both the hearing and the verdict. An open hearing may protect the reputation of the church in the community, particularly among those who might otherwise assume that the church had whitewashed the case in order to protect itself. Access also lessens the likelihood that the church will be the recipient of the kind of outcry that often greets the findings of inquiries that proceed behind closed doors, especially when a judgment of innocence is rendered by an all-clergy—perhaps even an all-*male* clergy—review panel.

Those directing the hearing may discover that they are torn by competing forces. On the one hand, they may understandably be reluctant to deal with personal and highly private matters in a public forum. On the other hand, they understand the compelling need to air such matters in the interest of justice. Their task is to handle the private details with delicacy, while ensuring that the information needed for a fair hearing emerges.

Step 4: Reaching Justice in the Formal Hearing

The panel of inquiry can anticipate several possible outcomes to their labors.

The charge may have actually been false, and the complainant may have been motivated by reasons that did not at first appear. If after carefully listening to the accuser, the panel reaches this conclusion, they must report their findings to the church and/or denominational leadership and conclude the process. In addition to exonerating the pastor, the process will have served a good purpose. Their judicious handling of the complaint will send a clear signal that the church takes allegations of sexual abuse seriously and that male gender and clergy power do not speak the last word in the Christian community.

The charge may be true and the pastor may be a predator. In this situation, the panel will likely face a prolonged and bitter battle in which the minister seeks to manipulate the process. Marie Fortune's account of Peter Donovan illustrates this. The struggle, which dragged out over three years, was filled with constant spiritual and psychological warfare. In the end no one came out unscathed. Few of the women whom Donovan had victimized and who bore the brunt of the ordeal received adequate pastoral care or experienced healing.[20] The repercussions of the matter nearly destroyed the church. The only positive result was the steps that the church and denomination took to rework their policies and procedures concerning clergy sexual misconduct and the cautionary lesson their experience has provided for the church as a whole. As Fortune notes, this incident stands as a stark reminder "that the church is responsible for the professional conduct of its clergy and must act to prevent misconduct from causing harm to its members or the community at large."[21]

If the accusation is true, the inquiry is more likely to produce a more amiable outcome. Confronted with his guilt, the pastor may desire to end the matter as quickly as possible. His concern is to learn what the consequences of his action will be. As we noted earlier, however, the inquiry ought not to close the matter too hurriedly. If the offense demands his resignation, or perhaps the suspension or withdrawal of his ordination, the panel must recommend to the governing body that they put proper support systems in place to help him through the coming dark days. Of all the events in his life, this will likely be the most traumatic.

If the offense is less serious and there are mitigating circumstances, the panel may recommend that the governing body consider a lesser penalty. But this requires the genuine repentance of the pastor, his willingness to submit to a program of supervision and discipline, and above all his remorseful attitude toward those he injured.

The least satisfactory result that the panel might anticipate is what Scottish courts call "Not Proven." In such circumstances the presumption of innocence demands that the panel absolve the pastor. While this ends the official inquiry, the panel may conclude that the pastor's professional habits are sorely in need of improvement, lest he someday fall into a more blatant act of indiscretion. In some cases, provision may need to be made for the pastor to change his ministry context.

In this situation the church ought to offer support to the complainant as well, even though her accusation was not proven. If her motives were pure, she likely stepped forward at great personal risk (she will surely face shame and ostracism), and therefore her courage deserves recognition.

Once they have reached a decision, the panel must immediately communicate its findings to all concerned parties, including the accused pastor, the complainant(s), the local church and the denominational leadership.

Step 5: Evaluating the Implications of Conviction

Conviction of a serious act of sexual failure that results in a pastor's dismissal and/or suspension of his ordination brings enormous consequences. Often those who go through this experience find themselves barely able to survive the emotional, spiritual, financial, familial, professional and personal toll that it extracts. As the Adventist minister we mentioned in chapter one reports, "Nothing prepared me for what was to follow."[22]

The church simply cannot hang their former pastor "out to dry," ignoring the personal and pastoral need that conviction poses. The church may continue to feel betrayed by their minister and therefore be in no mood for generosity. But once justice has been served, following Christ means focusing on mercy. To this end, the congregation or denomination can take several vital steps.

If he is married, one immediate concern must be the pastor's marriage and family. The church should seek to provide some type of marital and family counseling.

Perhaps the church's central concern is the restoration of the offending pastor to Christian fellowship and possible future service. If the perpetrator is a wanderer, the congregation should make every attempt to provide for his eventual participation in the life of the church—if not in the location where he served, then elsewhere. Whether and when he can resume some type of public ministry, however, depends on the policies of the church, the seriousness of the offense, his own repentance and an assessment of the impact of his behavior on the victims. As we noted in chapters one and five, an act of clergy sexual misconduct leaves many victims in its wake, including the complainant(s), spouses and family members, the local church and even the wider Christian community.

Courts of law in North America are increasingly turning to "victim impact statements" to assess the long-term repercussions of offenses involving victims. In the process of determining the appropriate penalty for an act, the court takes into account victims' descriptions of the effect the offense has had on their lives. The church could gain by incorporating this tool in its attempt to determine when—and if—a former pastor can be reinstated to a clergy role. The process of restoring a minister to his vocation would include the reception of updated victim impact statements. Both he and the church would listen to the ongoing consequences of his actions. These consequences would serve as one factor in determining whether or not his reinstatement is best for all parties concerned.

The premature restoration of a former pastor to leadership in the church is in nobody's interests. Such actions only serve to reinforce structures and perceptions that bias church life in favor of men and clergy. Thereby they maintain the very dynamics that have led to the church's present disastrous and disreputable situation.

But apart from considerations of the church's reputation in the world, premature restoration is not in the best interests of the pastor himself. Fuller

Seminary's publication *Focus* reminds us that "headline-making sexual escapades by high profile clergy are the tip of an iceberg of deep unresolved emotional and interpersonal issues of anger, loneliness, performance pressure and power hunger."[23] For this reason, restoration can never occur until the pastor has undergone sufficient counseling to uncover and resolve these deeper problems. To this must be added a genuine renewal of biblical spirituality, irrefutable evidence of an improved marital relationship (if he is married and his wife agrees to stay with him) and the construction of a long-term accountability and support system.

For some offenders, including predators, restoration to leadership and public ministry will likely never be possible. In such a situation the church should make no statement and take no action that even raises in the former minister's mind the expectation that he may one day return to the pastorate.

Apparently in an attempt to take this conclusion seriously, one denominational study paper on clergy sexual misconduct asserts, "Leaders with long standing patterns of sexual indiscretion or immorality may need a longer period of rehabilitation in their marriage and interaction and ministry."[24] However laudable the intent of its authors, their use of the word *may* represents the kind of thinking we find problematic and totally unacceptable. Can we anticipate that it will ever be in the best interests of the person with "a long standing pattern of sexual indiscretion or immorality" to consider the possibility of a future restoration to ministry? More importantly, could his return to leadership ever be in the interests of the church or the community? We wonder whether he ever met the New Testament standard for public leadership (1 Timothy 3:1-13; 1 Peter 2:11).

The church also must view the pastor's financial situation as both an immediate and a long-term concern. Immediately, the church should consider some type of short-term help. They may also provide the services of one of the reputable companies that counsel executives who lose their jobs. Finally, if the likelihood of his return to the pastorate is minimal, they must realize that he will need retraining.

Legal Concerns

Churches need to be aware that there are both civil and criminal implications involved in a sexual offense. Legal requirements vary in different countries, in states and provinces, and even in differing jurisdictions. Churches therefore need to be aware of the national, state and local rules governing their liability in cases of misconduct involving their employees.

One nearly universal requirement is the immediate reporting of any sexual misconduct involving minors. Typical is the British Columbia law declaring that it is "the legal duty of all persons to report immediately to the responsible agency situations in which they have reasonable grounds to believe that a child is in need of protection . . . failure to do so may constitute a summary offence (punishable by a $1,000.00 fine and/or six months in prison)."[25]

We live in a society where legal redress is becoming the norm. Victims of sexual misconduct are likewise increasingly likely to hold the church responsible for the actions of its staff, including launching legal proceedings against religious bodies.

In the United States, the courts have ruled against those denominations that have failed to act when they became aware of a problem involving their clergy. An important Colorado case in 1988 (*Destefano* v. *Grabian*) involved litigation against a Catholic priest and his diocese for alleged pastoral misconduct. The court's conclusion is significant: "The diocese could be legally accountable for the priest's actions if it was aware of previous occasions of similar misconduct involving the same priest and it failed to institute any means of supervising him." In reaching this conclusion, the court emphasized that denominations are not liable for the misconduct of clergy simply because of their relationship with each other. Liability occurs only if at the time of the misconduct the minister was acting within the scope of his or her employment, or if the denomination knew, or should have known, of previous acts of misconduct by the minister and it failed to enact any supervisory procedure.[26]

In Canada the Christian community has suffered considerable fallout from several notorious cases. The Roman Catholic Church, for example, has been bloodied legally and morally for what has been seen as a failure to take appropriate action when it was evident that church leaders were, or should have been, aware of cases of clergy sexual misconduct.

Whether guilty or innocent, the pastor may also hold the church legally responsible for its handling of his case. Because this remains a complicated matter in both the United States and Canada, each local church is well advised to check thoroughly its legal obligations as an employer. At the same time, because his claim to financial assistance may hang in the balance, a minister who ends his pastorate under a cloud must clearly know whether his resignation was voluntary or involuntary.

Involvement in a civil suit is never pleasant. Even if the church wins the case, the bills for legal counsel can cripple it financially. As a precaution, each church should explore the possibility of obtaining insurance to cover civil suits. In addition, every church should seek counsel from a lawyer who is familiar with church-state relationships. In view of the alarming growth of legal cases, churches must abandon their naivety regarding their legal jeopardy.

Sandy went to her pastor for counseling. Some time later, she accused him of taking advantage of her vulnerability and making sexual contact. The pastor admitted that he had been sexually involved with her and resigned from his position. Sandy, however, blamed the church for its lack of supervision of their pastor and asked for a modest amount of money to pay for the therapy she sensed she needed in order to recover from the experience. The church leadership, still reeling from the incident and indignant over her request, refused. Sandy filed suit. In the end, the costs the church incurred in the process of defending itself greatly exceeded Sandy's original request. And the loss of goodwill following the public disclosure of the behavior of their pastor and their apparent indifference to the victim was disastrous to the congregation.

Fear of legal reprisal and blatant self-interest may force churches to act generously toward victims of clergy sexual misconduct even in cases where they may not carry legal responsibility. But how much more compelling as a motivation for action should Christlike compassion be!

We concluded chapter six by alluding to Rutter's poignant comment: "Every forbidden-zone relationship in which sexual tension appears also presents an opportunity to heal. Because the man holds the balance of power, it is his responsibility to turn an impending sexual disaster into a healing moment. He must, for her sake, give up his sexual agenda toward her, once and for all. When he does this, he frees both of them to recover the abundant resources of the self."[27] A similar principle holds within the church. When the church gives up its own agenda, which focuses on its own survival as an institution, and begins to be genuinely caring toward those affected by clergy sexual misconduct, healing can begin.

8
Hope for
the Wanderer

In Tom's estimation, nothing positive or exciting was happening in the church in which he had been serving as pastor for the last five years. He had not only become bored and frustrated with the congregational ministry, but he was also losing his sense of call as a pastor. In the midst of his vocational crisis, Tom's wife, Sylvia, had to travel to another part of the country to settle her elderly parents into a care facility. This really did not matter much to Tom, however, for his relationship with Sylvia at this point was not good. It had been some time since he had felt passionate toward her. Actually, Tom was finding that almost nothing about life sparked his enthusiasm these days.

In his wife's absence, Tom began to spend time with Mary Lynn, an interesting and attractive member of his church. Mary Lynn seemed to like him and appeared to find his company enjoyable. She did not come on to him in any obvious manner; nevertheless, he sensed that she might be sexually available. For Tom, the relationship with Mary Lynn soon became the one bright spot in an otherwise dull existence, characterized by a church that was not particularly supportive of his work among them, a wife who was (understandably) more concerned about her parents at the moment than about him, and children who were preoccupied with their own lives. Tom began to fantasize about Mary Lynn. And he fed these fantasies by dabbling in a bit of pornography as well as making visits to Internet porn sites.

Tom never *intended* to act on his fantasies. But eventually his good intentions were not sufficient to prevent him from initiating physical contact with Mary Lynn. The two had a brief, intense sexual encounter. Almost immediately, however, both Tom and Mary Lynn felt appalled at what they had done and ashamed of their actions. They halted the affair. And they agreed to keep the matter a secret, to proceed as if nothing had happened.

To cope with his feelings of guilt and shame, Tom told himself that the fault was not really his. Mary Lynn had signaled to him her availability, Sylvia had put her parents before him, and the church was a serious disappointment. Furthermore, he reasoned, no real harm had been done. Tom decided that he would recommit himself to his marriage, his children, his church, and his Lord, and as a result all would be well.

In chapter two, we introduced the important distinction between the *wanderer* and the *predator*. In that context, we noted that the predator actively seeks opportunities to abuse women sexually with apparently little or no sense of appropriate personal moral restrictions. The wanderer, in contrast, does not *intend* to step over the boundary into the forbidden zone. Rather, we might say that he *falls* into sexual misconduct at a particularly vulnerable point in his life and ministry, such as in the wake of an overwhelming crisis or during a major transition in his life. Moreover, the predator's opportunistic approach means that he may likely be a repeat or multiple offender, whereas the wanderer may cross the line only once, especially if proper steps are taken to bring healing in his life.

The important distinctions that separate the wanderer from the predator lead to the question, Is there hope for the wanderer? What steps should be taken to insure that a wanderer does not develop into a predator? And how can a concerned pastor who senses his vulnerability but has not acted on such impulses safeguard his ministry so that he does not wander into the forbidden zone?

The Attitude of the Wanderer

We believe that by the grace of God there is indeed hope for the wanderer. Yet this hope does not emerge automatically. Instead, healing can come only if the wanderer's heart is softened through the experiences he faces so that he might be brought into a position to receive the divine grace available to him. The beginning point for this process lies with the wanderer's attitude.

Defending the wanderer. In the workshops we have conducted on the topic of clergy sexual misconduct, few if any of the participants have quarreled with the descriptions of the predator and the wanderer sketched in this book. Nor have attendees expressed any sympathy for the predator. Attitudes toward the wanderer, however, have often been quite different. We are convinced that if the wanderer is to gain a proper perspective regarding his situation, others must assist in the process. Their attitude toward the wanderer is often crucial in his own change of heart. How, then, should others in the fellowship, and especially other pastors, view the wanderer if healing is to be brought into his life?

Most characterizations of the wanderer portray this person as an "accidental" offender. The wanderer is generally not violent, nor is his sexual failure likely to be premeditated. Rather, temptation fells the wanderer at some particularly vulnerable point in his life. The vulnerability involved in such cases leads many people to express genuine sympathy for the wanderer. Such pity may be merely fear felt for oneself at the sight of another's distress, of course. Yet more often than not, expressions of sympathy are motivated by a genuine attempt to take seriously Paul's admonition, written, incidentally, in the context of sexual immorality: "If you think you are standing firm, be careful that you don't fall" (1 Cor. 10:12). Few if any male pastors want to be seen as overly judgmental concerning a matter that touches on their own vulnerability.

At the same time, menacing dangers lurk behind any outpouring of sympathy for the wanderer. An unguarded, overly sympathetic stance can all too readily lead to an inappropriate and ultimately counterproductive defense of a person who needs to take ownership of his attitudes and actions. Moreover, an unwillingness to confront the wanderer in the name of "not casting the first stone" can reinforce the wanderer's tendency to deny or minimize his sinful behavior. Defending the wanderer, therefore, can actually start him down the road to becoming a predator.

Evangelicals in England found themselves faced with a dilemma. A highly visible church leader terminated his ministry, left his wife and family and disappeared from the limelight. He did so because he wanted to pursue a relationship with a younger man in the congregation of which the well-known Christian leader was the pastor. This sad situation does not parallel exactly the situation of the wanderer as we have described it, nor was this pastor a predator. Nevertheless, the reaction the pastor's actions evoked from others is instructive in the context of our discussion of the wanderer. Christians who publicly commented on the situation found themselves torn between grief and anger. They wanted to understand and defend their fallen colleague, but they also found his conduct reprehensible. This sense of ambivalence was especially evident in a comment voiced within a fairly extensive critique of the case published in a popular Christian magazine. At one point in the essay, the author declared almost wistfully, "It is to the lonely and weary soul that the devil often comes in his gentlest and most persuasive guise."[1]

Reactions of sympathy born out of a fear of one's own vulnerability have their place, of course. Yet we do not do the wanderer a favor if we become sympathetic to the point of justifying his behavior. Defending the wanderer is simply not the way to bring about healing.

Blaming the other. In chapter five, we noted some of the chilling consequences that emerge once an incident of clergy sexual misconduct comes to light. Even under the best of circumstances, the affair will have repercussions for the pastor's relationship with his wife and his relationships with others within their family. It will also have long-term implications for his sexual partner, her husband and their family. And, of course, the effects will spiral outward to the church, the community and the denomination. For this reason, there will always be those who will urge the wanderer and the "other woman" to keep the affair secret. But even in situations in which this may be possible, such secrecy brings its own particular consequences. Family or personal secrets are the enemy of intimacy, and intimacy is the currency of any good marriage. Harboring a secret that could jeopardize one's marriage is bound to undermine the marital relationship from within. For this reason, a change in the wanderer's own attitude, and not his ability to keep the affair a secret, is what is required if healing is to come.

In the situation cited above, Tom clearly overlooked several crucial aspects of his involvement with Mary Lynn. Perhaps the most detrimental of these was the fact that he viewed the entire matter through the lens of a "blamer." Rather than admitting his own responsibility for what happened, Tom blamed other people: Mary Lynn, Sylvia and even the church. In his estimation, the wrong he committed was ultimately someone else's fault. Tom may not fit exactly the mold of the classic blamer delineated by Virginia Satir,[2] insofar as he is not loud and tyrannical. Nevertheless, he does exhibit several of the typical characteristics of a blamer that Satir outlines. If he were to articulate his attitude clearly, he might well say to everyone around him, "You are the responsible party; if it wasn't for you, everything would be all right."

Moreover, Tom struggles with his sense of worth, and the brief affair only served to intensify this struggle. In the end, Tom's failure to accept responsibility and his decision to blame someone else for his conduct enlarged rather than diminished his negative attitudes toward himself and others.

By blaming others, Tom may gain temporary relief from his feelings of guilt. But becoming a blamer is never the solution to the problem a wanderer faces. By pointing the finger at someone else, Tom only forestalls the real healing that he needs. Such healing can come only when he deals with his own sin, when he takes ownership over his actions, and thereby places himself in a position to receive forgiveness and gain release from the genuine guilt he carries. Moreover, rather than preparing him to face future crises, blaming others will only feed the unhealthy coping pattern that he is developing. If allowed to go unchecked, this pattern of blaming others may ultimately start Tom down the road to becoming a predator.

Setting out on the road to healing. The attitude of a pastor who has wandered into the forbidden zone is crucial. He must avoid listening to the voices that offer an uncritical, categorical defense of his actions. And he must resist his own tendency to blame others for his actions. Instead of defending and blaming, the wanderer needs humbly to acknowledge his own complicity and take the steps necessary to get the help he so desperately needs.

One potentially rich source of help for a wanderer like Tom is a spiritual director. In Tom's situation, the basic role of a spiritual director is to assist him in the process of gaining a proper perspective of his attitudes, actions and reactions. An astute spiritual director would be able to lead Tom to probe beneath the mere surface issues by challenging his erroneous and superficial views regarding the causes of, and forces at work in, not only his sexual misconduct but also his resultant attitude toward it. The goal of spiritual direction is to lead Tom to a new understanding of the core spiritual realities with which he must come to grips if true healing is to occur, including the central biblical dynamics of guilt and grace. A spiritual director would also help Tom work through the crucial congregational and denominational dimensions of the situation in which he is enmeshed.

Perhaps the most immediate task of the spiritual director, however, would be to foster in Tom a proper attitude toward his marriage and to instill in him not only the desire to rediscover a good marriage but a vibrant hope that this can indeed occur. Tom will especially need assistance as he struggles with the task of confessing his failure to Sylvia. He will need to come to grips with the fact that his marriage will never be the same again. Confessing his adultery to his wife will not inevitably lead to divorce. Nor will his actions necessitate a permanently injured relationship with his wife if the marriage survives. Confession will, however, alter their marriage. Not only can a spiritual director forewarn Tom of this, but he or she can walk with the couple through the days that follow the revelation of sexual infidelity. This person can help facilitate the renewal of their relationship by working with Tom in the painful task of coming to grips with what it means to admit sin and experience forgiveness in this situation. In walking with the couple, the spiritual director stands as a sign of hope, especially for Tom, who needs to believe that he can emerge from this process a better and stronger husband and father. In addition, Tom may need to gain a sense of hope that the process may eventually make him a better pastor as well, should his denomination be willing to work with him toward this end.

Experiencing Marriage Encounter. Tom needs to undergo a transformation in attitude that overcomes his tendency to look for scapegoats to blame for his actions. One crucial means of conquering this debilitating tendency is to focus his attention once again on his own marriage and to do his part in rekindling the kind of relationship with his wife that God intends for them to share. The likelihood of a pastor falling into an extramarital relationship to begin with, and also therefore of becoming a predator, is lessened dramatically if he makes a commitment to take the lead in constantly renewing his marriage.

When some of the dust has settled, therefore, Tom will need to gain a fresh perspective on his marriage. To this end, he might well propose to Sylvia that they attend a Marriage Encounter seminar.

Actually, a Marriage Encounter seminar is not only for couples who are going through difficult times. It can serve as "preventive medicine" for almost any pastor's marriage by helping the couple keep their marriage from growing stale and becoming boring for both partners, thereby helping them avoid the temptation of blaming the other. On the basis of its research, the National Institute of the Family has concluded that Marriage Encounter "is a positive marriage enrichment experience for nine out of ten couples."[3] This observation has been confirmed by the testimony of many attendees. Michael McManus, to cite one enthusiastic proponent, waxes lyrical about the effects he and his wife experienced: "After a decade of marriage, we fell back in love with one another, but at a more profound level than anything we had experienced before."[4] He then adds, "The impact of the weekend has been permanent, because we learned a new form of soul to soul communication that has deepened and enriched each day of our marriage in the seventeen years since."[5]

James Dobson attended a seminar with his wife, Shirley, primarily for "professional reasons." To his surprise it afforded them, in his words, "the opportunity to occasion the deepest, most intimate exchange of feelings we had known in 20 years," and thereby "it proved to be one of the highlights of my life."[6] As a result, Dobson now recommends the experience to others: "I just wish that everyone who trusts my opinion would now accept this advice. Attend a Marriage Encounter weekend at the earliest opportunity."[7]

We would take Dobson's recommendation a step farther. We are convinced that the pressures that come to bear on pastors' marriages are of such magnitude that credentialing bodies ought to make attendance at a Marriage Encounter seminar or its equivalent mandatory for all clergy couples. Of course, by no means should this stipulation be viewed as a magical cure. Nor is it the sole answer to the problem of clergy sexual misconduct. Nevertheless, we believe that participation in a marriage enriching seminar is the single most important step one can take to reduce the risk this debilitating threat poses to the life of the church today.

Growing a Good Marriage

The workshops in which we have been involved have opened our eyes to the dismaying lack of information among pastors regarding what constitutes a good marriage and how to grow one. To be sure, Christians routinely exhort one another in this matter. And Christians incessantly debate the question of the roles of husbands and wives. Yet, Christians in general and pastors in particular are largely ignorant about the actual dynamics of a wholesome, God-honoring marriage.

Help for marriages. In addition to the wealth of Christian books on the topic of marriage, Christians do well to learn from the insights of experts writing from the perspective of contemporary marriage psychology. Vastly superior in this regard to the popular books written by John Gray is the work of John Gottman. His two important books, *Why Marriages Succeed or Fail* [8] and *The Seven Principles for Making Marriage Work,* [9] are essential reading for a pastor's well-being and ministry.

Gottman is the first person to attempt to apply laboratory techniques to the study of marriage. His basic conclusion comes as no great surprise: "If there is one lesson I have learned from my years of research it is that a lasting marriage results from a couple's ability to resolve the conflicts that are inevitable in any marriage." [10] But how should they go about resolving conflict? Gottman has determined that there is no one right way to do so. Rather, he notes that there are different styles of resolving conflict and that all of these are equally valid. What *is* vital, however, is finding the right balance between positive and negative interactions. Gottman asserts unambiguously, "Amazingly, we have found that it all comes down to a simple mathematical formula: no matter what style your marriage follows, you must have at least five times as many positive as negative moments together if your marriage is to be stable."[11]

The crucible of pastoral life works against maintaining the proper balance that Gottman outlines. Ministry often sets up a situation in which the dynamics of blame all too easily take over. Gottman asserts that a marriage is undermined if the partners give place to what he denotes as "the Four Horsemen of the Apocalypse."[12] These relationship-wrecking intruders usually "clip-clop into the heart of the marriage in the following order: criticism, contempt, defensiveness and stonewalling."[13]

Gottman's insights take us back to Tom's situation. Although we know little about the downward spiral that robbed Tom and Sylvia's marriage of health and vitality, we can safely conjecture that the difficulties did not suddenly emerge when Tom first fantasized about Mary Lynn. No doubt Tom's sense of boredom, frustration and loss of a sense of call invaded their marriage long before Sylvia went to help her parents move to the care facility. And Tom's failure to take the warning signs seriously became an invitation to trouble. Their marriage was ripe for the invasion of Gottman's "Four Horsemen" of the marital apocalypse. When the warning signs first began to cloud the horizon was the time for Tom to open up to his wife, so that together they could weather the storm that his looming crisis of vocation was fomenting.

Dealing with the pressures of a clergy marriage. The person who is often left out in discussions of the wanderer is the pastor's wife. As we noted earlier in this volume, she (like the other woman) is all too often regarded as a cause of the pastor's downfall. Stated simply, the pastor's wife often becomes the scapegoat. This attitude of blaming the pastor's wife not only allows the wanderer to rationalize his sinful behavior, but it overlooks the difficulty of her role. Cameron Lee and Jack

Balswick discuss what it is like to be married to a minister. They point out how complicated the role of a minister's wife has become:

> The role of the pastor's wife can be as complex as the pastor's. She, too, is often expected to fulfill superhuman expectations. These may both exhaust her and isolate her from the kind of friendships she needs to cope with the stress. Beyond this, the changing roles of women in society in general can add confusion to her already complicated role decisions. The clergy wife must develop ways of coping with her role stress that do not encourage either triangling or social withdrawal.[14]

The difficulties with which pastors and their spouses must cope extend to the very heart of their marriage. Family Systems practitioners argue, rather colorfully, that there are six people in the marital bed. In addition to the couple there are both sets of parents (which for most people is not a reassuring thought). In the case of clergy marriage, however, the situation is even more complex. In a marriage in which one of the partners is a pastor, the number of persons who share the marital bed grows from six to seven. The additional participant is the church. And the church does not make for a good bed companion.

Researchers disagree about the quality of clergy marriages today. Lee and Balswick conclude, "At present we have more reason to believe that the majority of clergy couples are happy rather than unhappy."[15] Many, however, would question this assessment. Indeed, many persons who have left the pastorate testify that their marriages improved as a result of their vocational transition. Ex-pastors, in other words, report that kicking the church out of the marital bed had a positive impact on the marriage relationship. Even former pastors who considered their marital relationships to be good found their family situations happier or greatly improved when they left the ministry. And they report that the change of occupation, not the individual family situation, was the cause of this improvement.[16]

It is hardly a matter of dispute that the pastoral vocation increases the pressure on a marriage. And in a problematic situation, such as that of Tom and Sylvia, the church often compounds the marital difficulties experienced. At the same time, clergy couples do not need to be mindless victims of what at first glance appears to be a potentially complicating context. In the end, the marriage partners are responsible for their actions. Furthermore, there are healthy steps a clergy couple can take to strengthen their marriage. These include attending a Marriage Encounter seminar, learning to pray together and even seeking out a competent marriage counselor. Moreover, the couple might consider ways in which they can enlist the support of the church in this task, knowing that no congregation willingly and willfully sets out to be a detriment to the health of the marital relationship of their pastor and his wife. Taking our cue from Gottman's findings, the key is to maintain a healthy balance of positive marital experiences so that the relationship is able to weather the strains that will inevitably arise.

Spiritual intimacy in the pastor's marriage. An obvious but routinely overlooked component of any healthy clergy marriage is the spiritual bond between husband and wife. Many researchers have confirmed that a significant connection exists among spiritual intimacy, physical intimacy and the capacity for intimacy in general. In fact, a leading book in this field, Frank Pittman's *Private Lies*, is aptly subtitled *Infidelity and the Betrayal of Intimacy*.[17]

Tom's loss of passion for Sylvia entails a veiled complaint about what he perceived as a lack of intimacy in his marriage. Unfortunately, rather than taking positive steps to rekindle his marital relationship, he looked for intimacy in the wrong place. Any number of resources could have guided Tom in wholesome directions. For example, he could have learned from Clifford and Joyce Penner, who "help couples restore the pleasure to their sex lives by helping them improve their communication, by educating them about each other's sexual response, and by guiding them through the sexual retraining process."[18] But beyond the physical dimension of their relationship, Tom and Sylvia appear to need an infusion of intimacy in every aspect of their lives, especially the spiritual.

According to Donald Harvey, Tom and Sylvia's case is not an isolated one. On the contrary, he finds the lack of spiritual intimacy in pastoral marriages disturbing.[19] In support of his contention, Harvey quotes these words from a pastor's wife who bemoans the lack of the spiritual dimension in her marriage: "We're just not close spiritually! We never have been. This good spiritual man won't pray with me. He won't have devotions with me. He won't even talk to me about spiritual matters of any kind."[20] Indeed, there is ample anecdotal evidence to suggest that pastors who pray with their wives are the exception rather than the rule.

Harvey is convinced that there is appallingly meager spiritual intimacy in today's Christian marriages.[21] But what is spiritual intimacy? Harvey offers what he calls a "practical and descriptive" account of it. In his estimation, it entails "being able to *share* your spiritual self, find this *reciprocated,* and having a *sense* of union with your mate."[22] He then adds, "Based on this definition, spiritual intimacy is something that we *do,* something that we *feel,* and something that is *interactional.*"[23] Having rightly argued that we are created for intimacy, he continues, "You can have all the dimensions of closeness (emotional, intellectual, sexual, social, and recreational), but if you are lacking the spiritual, you are really missing out. Nothing else so enhances a marriage." Consequently, he urges couples to commit themselves to fostering spiritual intimacy in their marriage, knowing that "it is always worth the effort to have all that God intends."[24]

Tom and Sylvia drifted apart in their marriage doubtlessly for a variety of reasons. Spending time on a regular basis reading Scripture and praying together will not cure all that ails their marriage. On the contrary, if they now look to such practices as the cure-all or use them as a way of glossing over or denying the deeply embedded, long-standing issues they must face, the superficial quest for spiritual intimacy could possibly work to their detriment, even precipitating the eventual total breakdown of their marriage. Nevertheless, without the restoration of spiritual intimacy to their marriage, one or the other will be left feeling increasingly spiritually destitute.

For Tom, the risks of opening himself to a deep level of spiritual intimacy with Sylvia are considerable. However, if he fails to begin the process, his risks are even greater. In Tom's situation, the alternative to a growing spiritual intimacy with Sylvia is the likelihood of coming to view his relationship with her, as well as their marriage itself, as just another dead weight pulling him under. If that becomes the case, he will find it difficult to resist the temptation to cut loose from it all. Although ending the marriage may give him an immediate sense of relief, when the temporary euphoria subsides, he will discover to his dismay that there is little left to his life. Reconnecting spiritually could be the way not only of avoiding that tragic scenario but also of revitalizing their marriage and his—and their—ministry as well.

Heading Off Danger

Frank Pittman offers some sobering words for Tom and every other actual or potential wanderer:

> It should be apparent that infidelity can cause all manner of problems, some immediate, some generations later. One would think people would know that by now. Nonetheless, every time people commit an infidelity and all hell breaks loose, they look so surprised. Even after twenty-seven years as a psychiatrist and family therapist, devoting much of my time to cleaning up the emotional mess after other people's affairs, I never cease to wonder at the naivete of people going through it.[25]

Pittman's perspective stands as a reminder that we do the wanderer no favor if we suggest to him that his extramarital affair is understandable and largely excusable. The way forward for the wanderer is to eschew the tendency to rationalize his behavior by blaming others. Instead, he must accept responsibility for his actions; seek out the help that he (and those he has affected) will need in order to work through the process of confession, forgiveness and healing; and set in motion the dynamic that can lead to a revitalization of his life, marriage and perhaps eventually his ministry as well. If the fallen pastor is willing to move forward in this manner, humbly and with his heart transformed under the disciplinary oversight of the Holy Spirit, there is hope for the wanderer.

We have outlined one crucial dimension of this process. Hope for the wanderer arises out of a commitment to one's marriage and a concerted effort to keep it fresh and vibrant. But the pastor's marriage is not the only dimension of the wanderer's situation that must be taken seriously. Consequently, in addition to building a strong marriage, there are other crucial ingredients in the hope-filled process. And these ingredients apply not only to the pastor who has wandered into the forbidden zone but also to the potential wanderer.

Accepting personal responsibility. We have noted that the all-too-common reaction of the wanderer is to blame others for his misguided actions. This climate of blaming almost invariably nurtures the tendency to excuse oneself by pointing to one's debilitating circumstances. The wanderer routinely voices the claim that he would not have behaved as he did if he had not found himself in the midst of an exceptionally difficult combination of circumstances. Although extenuating circumstances often do add a degree of pressure, circumstances are never the ultimate cause of a person's actions.

The wanderer's readiness to excuse his conduct by appeal to circumstances indicates that he has not yet come to the point at which he is prepared to accept responsibility for his own choices and behavior. In the process of getting out of the trap laid by the blame-syndrome, the wanderer can gain help from the findings of people such as Albert Ellis.[26]

Although Ellis's ideas on religion and what constitutes irrational ideas are highly suspect, the "ABC theory" of personality he promotes is applicable to the situation of the wanderer. This theory charts a progression from the activating event ("A") to the individual's beliefs and values ("B") leading to the emotional and behavioral consequences ("C").

Tom's response to his affair with Mary Lynn suggests that he would likely argue that the activating event—Sylvia's absence and Mary Lynn's availability—led directly to "C," the emotional and behavioral consequences. Ellis, however, would strongly dispute Tom's appraisal of the process. According to ABC theory, the activating event kicked in "B," namely, Tom's own beliefs and values. These, in turn, triggered "C."

The ABC appraisal of Tom's situation reveals that the wanderer (and the potential wanderer) truly needs to undergo a change in belief system. According to Ellis, "Human beings are largely responsible for creating their own emotional reactions and disturbances." The way forward, therefore, is to show people "how they can change the irrational beliefs that directly cause their disturbed emotional consequences."[27] In Tom's case, the belief that needs altering centers on his perception that he is alone. Indeed, Tom gives the distinct impression that he is lonely, despite the fact that he is married, has children and serves as the pastor of a church. For whatever reason, none of his relationships is able to provide the antidote to his feelings of isolation and loneliness. In addition, however, Tom likely reinforces his sense of loneliness with a variety of negative impressions about himself and others that he has internalized. He probably tells himself that he's bound to feel unhappy because he's alone and isn't getting enough love and attention.

In short, what a person believes has enormous consequences, not merely intellectually, but also emotionally and behaviorally. Tom's erroneous beliefs about himself and others set him up for failure. When the opportunity to engage in an illicit sexual affair emerged, the beliefs he had built up over the preceding months or even years led him astray.

If Tom is to escape from the emotional consequences of this downward spiral, he will need to identify these negative thought patterns and find constructive, life-affirming and, above all, biblical alternatives to them. At first glance, this appears to be a tall order. Yet it can be done. The key, however, is to attack head-on the negative, distorted thinking that is so destructive to people like Tom. Tom (as well as the potential wanderer) needs to remind himself of the simple fact that he is loved—by others and ultimately by God. Hence, the negative, destructive thoughts that plague him can be dispelled with a true appraisal of his situation: "I am not alone. There are people who will gladly give me both love and attention. Supremely, I am loved by God in Christ."

The highly successful Alcoholics Anonymous program was built on the supposition that persons must guard the way they think if they are to avoid being vulnerable to disaster. Actually, Jesus himself made the same point when he said, "For out of the heart come evil thoughts, murder, adultery, sexual immorality, theft, false testimony, slander" (Matt. 15:19). It is precisely in the realm of the heart—which includes one's core, operative beliefs about God, oneself and others—that the battle is won or lost. If the potential wanderer loses this battle of the heart, he will almost certainly lose the battle elsewhere. But if pastors maintain healthy beliefs at the core of their being, they put themselves in a good position to gain the victory over the temptation to look for intimacy in the wrong places.

Setting ministry boundaries. Another difficulty that starts some pastors down the path to becoming a wanderer is the inability to maintain healthy boundaries within their ministry. In fact, for many pastors, the overwhelming sense of stress they experience arises to a large degree precisely at this point. They either fail to understand what constitutes proper boundaries in their ministry, or they are simply unable to preserve such boundaries. Their own emotional needs overpower their judgment to such an extent that they do not know how or when to say no.

Jack prided himself on his availability. He owned all the latest gadgets that enabled anyone who desired to contact him to do so wherever he was and whenever a need arose. The congregation mistook his readiness to be at their beck and call for a deep love for each of them personally, for the church as a whole and, above all, for the Lord. So did Jack.

Because of Jack's availability, he was always tired. Furthermore, neither his wife nor his children could ever rely on having his undivided attention. Family picnics, the kids' sports events, birthdays, anniversaries, even holidays and vacations were always conditional—held hostage to the needs of the congregation—and subject to be interrupted or even terminated if a perceived emergency arose. Jack simply did not believe that he could set limits on his ministry and still claim to be a loving, caring pastor.

Jack is traveling the well-worn pathway to defeat. Somewhere down the road, Jack may discover to his dismay that he has lost his wife and family. Even if his marriage remains intact, his unhealthy inability to set boundaries for his ministry will have taken its toll. He may one day wake up to the fact that his indifference toward his children has driven them away from him. And he may eventually find that even his own sense of satisfaction in ministry has vanished, having been dislodged by an anger and resentment born from his perception that the recipients of his self-sacrificial ministry have taken him and his selflessness for granted. Henry Cloud and John Townsend describe the debilitating dynamic at work here: "Throughout the Scriptures, people are reminded of their choices and asked to take responsibility for them. . . . Making decisions based on others' approval or on guilt breeds resentment, a product of our sinful nature. We have been so trained by others on what we should do, that we think we are being loving when we do things out of compulsion."[28]

The longer Jack maintains the pattern of ministering without boundaries the less productive he is likely to become. In addition, his sense of loss will increase. Even if his untiring labors produce what he believes is a successful church, his "ministry approval ratings" will turn out to be a poor compensation for the losses he now senses, namely, the loss of marriage and family, as well as his own inner pain and disillusionment that have occasioned a loss of meaning in his life. Moreover, Jack is a prime candidate for becoming an unintentional wanderer.

Is there hope for Jack? Can he forestall what appears to be the inevitable? Yes. But to arrest this downward plunge, Jack needs to sit down with his wife, Ann, and talk about what is going on. He needs to own both his compulsive behavior and its unhealthy motivation. He must admit that attempting to please everyone is not only impossible but detrimental.

Furthermore, it will likely be difficult for Jack to wean the congregation off the bad habits he has encouraged over the years of "unboundaried" ministry, but it is imperative that he begin the process. A good first step will be to replace his pager and cell phone with a good answering service, which can buy him the space needed to sort out the urgent from what can wait. And of course he must take back from the congregation the time that he should be investing in his marriage and his family. Here again the potential wanderer needs to be proactive. Playing the role of the dedicated victim will ultimately not work.

But does setting boundaries turn the dedicated pastor from the others-centered attitude so crucial for effective ministry? Does the pastor risk becoming self-centered in the process of saying no? According to Cloud and Townsend, the opposite is in fact true. In their estimation, "Appropriate boundaries actually increase our ability to care about others. People with highly developed limits are the most caring people on earth."[29] Although they may be guilty of hyperbole, Cloud and Townsend offer an interesting perspective when they posit a close connection between the ability to set healthy boundaries and truly caring for others. At the very least, Cloud and Townsend dispel the erroneous belief that potential wanderers such as Jack often carry around with them, namely, that the lack of limits is a sign of genuine godliness. Contrary to what Jack and others may believe, the inability to set boundaries may well be rooted in an unhealthy family of origin, where attention, affection and approval were missing. Consequently, what Jack may believe is a sign of his devotion to Christ and to Christ's church may in fact be the product of his own deep-seated emotional disorder.

Avoiding workaholism. The other issue that needs addressing in the attempt to head off the potential wanderer and stop the one-time offender from becoming a predator is workaholism, which of course shares much in common with the inability to set healthy boundaries. Barbara Killinger describes a workaholic as "a person who gradually becomes emotionally crippled and addicted to control and power in a compulsive drive to gain approval and success."[30] She goes so far as to declare that "work is a substitute 'religious' experience for many workaholics."[31]

If Killinger is correct, the workaholic who appears highly motivated and unquestionably committed to the Lord and to the church is actually motivated by the worship of approval and success. This means that the workaholic is neither psychologically nor spiritually healthy. And the results are potentially disastrous. Because workaholism starves intimacy, it has become a major cause of marital breakdown. As the marriage deteriorates, the vulnerability of the workaholic pastor increases. Although an affair may well be the last thing the pastor desires, through his workaholic behavior pattern he has in fact put himself in a vulnerable position and has increased the odds of stepping over the line. Killinger urges the workaholic to recognize how troubled he is and to enlist both professional help and family support in the process of change.

To conclude, in this chapter we have engaged the question, Is there hope for the wanderer? Actually, this question embodies two queries: Must the pastor who has an affair inevitably become a repeat offender? And must the potential wanderer inevitably step over the line? Our answer to both is a resounding no. There is indeed hope for the (potential) wanderer. But such hope does not arise automatically. To a large degree it is dependent on the voices to which the pastor himself chooses to listen and the steps toward healing and wholeness he willingly takes.

There is little hope for the (potential) wanderer who listens to those inner and outer voices that offer only the kind of hollow sympathetic words that excuse sinful behavior, allow him to blame others and gingerly avoid raising the deeper issues in his life that are endangering his marriage and his ministry. Whatever the extenuating circumstances may be that eventually trigger an affair, the (potential) wanderer's troubles began long before any overt sexual misconduct occurred. The wanderer can only hope for healing if he is willing to admit these deeper-lying troubles and face them head-on. And to face these problems squarely, the hopeful (potential) wanderer must enlist the support of a network of people who will relate to him honestly, with integrity, and lovingly. Not only can these supportive persons provide the dose of accountability that can serve to keep the (potential) wanderer from falling into temptation, they can themselves become a sign of hope, for they stand against the sense of loneliness and despair that lie just beneath the surface of us all as we travel the pilgrim highway.

As the (potential) wanderer resolves to be proactive in the process of constructive change, he will discover anew the transformative power of the Holy Spirit, who not only changes the heart but is the divine power needed to change one's entire life. By the power of the Spirit, there is hope that the (potential) wanderer can indeed live in a manner that brings honor to the God who has called him into the glorious service of Christ.

Appendix
A Checkup for the Wanderer (Real or Potential)

1. Do you blame everyone else for what is wrong or seriously inef-
    fective in your life?
    Yes_____   No_____
2. Do you in practice reject the idea of a personal spiritual direc-
    tor/mentor who is mature enough to hold you responsible and
    facilitate change in your life?
    Yes_____   No_____
3. When your spouse wants you to join her in a Marriage Encounter
    seminar, do you find excuses to avoid this?
    Yes_____   No_____
4. When you read John Gottman's ideas about marriage, do you
    dismiss them as unnecessary and as having little to offer you in
    your marriage?
    Yes_____   No_____
5. When you talk to yourself are you preoccupied with negative
    thoughts and beliefs?
    Yes_____   No_____

6. Do you see your wife and the church as two more burdens you have to bear?

    Yes_____   No_____

7. Do you fantasize about sexual involvement outside your marriage and find such fantasies more attractive than your marriage?

    Yes_____   No_____

8. Does your family complain about the lack of healthy boundaries in your professional life?

    Yes_____   No_____

9. Are approval and success what you dream about, and will you pay any price to achieve them?

    Yes_____   No_____

10. Do you reject the idea that you need to develop a commitment to deeper spirituality?

    Yes_____   No_____

Answering yes to any of these questions indicates that you are vulnerable to becoming a wanderer, and the greater number of yes answers, the greater the potential for misconduct. On the other hand, every yes answer that is subsequently changed to no is an encouraging move in a healthy direction.

The wanderer must not settle for even one yes answer. Of course, the path you must travel to change a yes to a no will be a major emotional and spiritual challenge. However, the rewards of taking up the challenge are even greater, for this process promises a reinvigorated marriage and both spiritual and professional health for you as a pastor.

Notes

Introduction

[1]Gail Sherman, "Behind Closed Doors: Therapist-Client Sex," *Psychology Today*, May/June 1993, pp. 64-81.

[2]Ibid., p. 65.

[3]Paul Taylor, *The Globe and Mail*, April 2, 1991, p. A4.

[4]Imber Black, *Secrets in Families and Family Therapy* (New York: Norton, 1993), p. 13.

[5]Ibid., p. 14.

[6]Peter Rutter, *Sex in the Forbidden Zone: When Men in Power—Therapists, Doctors, Clergy, Teachers and Others—Betray Women's Trust* (Los Angeles: Jeremy P. Tarcher, 1986), p. 16.

[7]Ibid., p. 11.

[8]Ibid., p. 21.

[9]Ibid.

[10]Ibid., p. 24.

[11]Ibid., p. 40.

[12]Ibid., p. 20.

[13]Ibid., p. 17.

[14]Sherman, "Behind Closed Doors," p. 67.

[15]"Preventing Family Violence" (Vancouver: British Columbia Council for the Family, 1993), p. 1.

[16]Because clergy sexual misconduct constitutes an abuse of power as well as a sexual

failure, and because power is still a male preserve, we can assume that what applies to family violence also applies to sexual misconduct in the church family, which we will argue is a form of family violence.

Chapter 1: The Scope of the Problem

[1]*Christian Info News* 13 (October 1993): 5.

[2]Thomas S. Giles, "Coping with Sexual Misconduct in the Church," *Christianity Today* 27 (January 11, 1993): 49.

[3]Joan Clayton, "My Minister Kept Making Passes," *Ladies Home Journal* 102 (July 1985): 16, 20.

[4]Debra Fieguth, "After All These Years," *Faith Today*, March/April 1994, p. 29.

[5]Peter Rutter, *Sex in the Forbidden Zone: When Men in Power—Therapists, Doctors, Clergy, Teachers and Others—Betray Women's Trust* (Los Angeles: Jeremy P. Tarcher, 1989), p. 36.

[6]David Rice, *Shattered Vows: Exodus from the Priesthood* (Belfast: Blackstaff, 1990), p. 3.

[7]A. W. Richard Sipe, *A Secret World: Sexuality and the Search for Celibacy* (New York: Brunner/Mazel, 1990), p. 74.

[8]Bob Harvey, "Sexual Harassment," *Vancouver Sun*, March 31, 1992, p. A14.

[9]The survey was conducted by Richard Blackman for a Ph.D. dissertation at Fuller Theological Seminary. These results are cited in John D. Vogelsang, "From Denial to Hope: A Systemic Response to Clergy Sexual Abuse," *Journal of Religion and Health* 32 (Fall 1993): 197.

[10]Karen Lebacqz and Ronald G. Barton, *Sex in the Parish* (Louisville, Ky.: Westminster/ John Knox, 1991), p. 71.

[11]"People and Events, Briefly Noted," *Christianity Today* 36 (September 14, 1992): 63.

[12]Julia Duin, "Renewal Leader Pulkingham Admits Guilt," *Christianity Today* 36 (September 14, 1992): 78.

[13]Flynn Ritchie, *Christian Info News,* October 1992, p. M3.

[14]Responses to these two questions were reported and discussed in "How Common Is Pastoral Indiscretion?" *Leadership* 9 (Winter 1988): 12-13.

[15]Jeff T. Seat, James T. Trent and Jwa K. Kim, "The Prevalence and Contributing Factors of Sexual Misconduct Among Southern Baptist Pastors in Six Southern States," *Journal of Pastoral Care* 47 (Winter 1993): 365.

[16]Herbert S. Strean, *Therapists Who Have Sex with Their Patients: Treatment and Recovery* (New York: Brunner/Mazel, 1993), p. 2.

[17]Ibid., p. 4.

[18]Vogelsang, "From Denial to Hope," p. 199.

[19]Gordon MacDonald, *Rebuilding Your Broken World* (Nashville: Oliver Nelson, 1988), p. 11.

[20]Lebacqz and Burton, *Sex in the Parish,* pp. 224-25.

[21]Annette Lawson, *Adultery: An Analysis of Love and Betrayal* (New York: Basic Books,

1988), p. 221.

[22]Ibid, p. 222.

[23]For a lengthier discussion of this phenomenon, see Stanley J. Grenz, *Sexual Ethics* (Dallas: Word, 1990), pp. 81-98.

[24]Frank Pittman, "Behind Closed Doors: Therapist-Client Sex," *Psychology Today,* May/June 1993, p. 82.

[25]College of Physicians and Surgeons of Ontario, *The Preliminary Report of the Task Force on Sexual Abuse of Patients* (1991), p. 12.

[26]Ibid.

[27]Rutter, *Sex in the Forbidden Zone,* p. 30.

[28]Janice Russell, *Out of Bounds: Sexual Exploitation in Counselling and Therapy* (London: Sage, 1993), p. 17. Russell cites a 1986 study conducted by Pope and Bouthoutsos.

[29]Pamela Cooper-White, "Soul Stealing: Power and Relations in Pastoral Sexual Abuse," *The Christian Century* 108 (February 20, 1991): 197.

[30]For a succinct description of this phenomenon, see G. Lloyd Rediger, *Ministry and Sexuality* (Minneapolis: Fortress, 1990), p. 29.

[31]Marie Fortune, *Is Nothing Sacred?* (San Francisco: Harper & Row, 1989), p. 110-11.

Chapter 2: The Pastor at Risk

[1]Roger Bryant, "I Committed Adultery," *Ministry* 65 (July 1992): 13.

[2]Ibid., p. 11.

[3]Peter Rutter, *Sex in the Forbidden Zone: When Men in Power—Therapists, Doctors, Clergy, Teachers and Others—Betray Women's Trust* (Los Angeles: Jeremy P. Tarcher, 1989), p. 11.

[4]See J. Steven Muse, "Faith, Hope and the 'Urge to Merge' in Pastoral Ministry: Some Countertransference-Related Distortions of Relationships Between Male Pastors and Their Female Parishioners," *Journal of Pastoral Care* 46 (Fall 1992): 302-3. Brock and Lukens list six personality types that are especially at risk. Raymond T. Brock and Horace C. Lukens Jr., "Affair Prevention in the Ministry," *Journal of Psychology and Christianity* 8 (1989): 45-46.

[5]Marie M. Fortune, *Is Nothing Sacred? When Sex Invades the Pastoral Relationship* (San Francisco: Harper & Row, 1992), p. 47.

[6]Ibid., p. 104.

[7]Ibid., p. 156.

[8]Ibid.

[9]Ibid.

[10]Cameron Lee and Jack Balswick, *Life in a Glass House* (Grand Rapids, Mich.: Zondervan, 1989), p. 197.

[11]Karen Lebacqz and Ronald G. Barton, *Sex in the Parish* (Louisville, Ky.: Westminster/John Knox, 1991), p. 129.

[12]Rutter, *Sex in the Forbidden Zone,* p. 25.

[13]Janice Russell, *Out of Bounds: Sexual Exploitation in Counselling and Therapy* (London: Sage, 1993), p. 98.

[14]Cited in ibid., pp. 110-11.

[15]Lebacqz and Barton, *Sex in the Parish*, p. 131.

[16]Ibid., p. 188.

[17]Pamela Cooper-White, "Soul Stealing: Power and Relations in Pastoral Sexual Abuse," *The Christian Century* 108 (February 20, 1991): 198.

[18]Thoburn and Balswick differentiate between necessary causes ("those characteristics which comprise the historical, interpersonal, and intra-psychic life of the pastor, which . . . form the basis for sexual temptation") and sufficient causes ("the lack of safeguards existing within the ministerial role, which . . . create the seedbed for sexual temptation"). John Thoburn and Jack O. Balswick, "A Prevention Approach to Infidelity Among Male Protestant Clergy," *Pastoral Psychology* 42 (1993): 46-47.

[19]J. W. Thoburn, "Predictive Factors Regarding Extra-marital Sexual Activity Among Male Protestant Clergy," Ph.D. dissertation, Fuller Theological Seminary, 1991, as cited in Thoburn and Balswick, "Prevention Approach," p. 47.

[20]Thoburn and Balswick, "Prevention Approach," p. 47. The authors credit the idea to M. F. Schwartz.

[21]Peter L. Steinke, "Clergy Affairs," *Journal of Psychology and Christianity* 8 (1989): 56-62.

[22]"How Common Is Pastoral Indiscretion?" *Leadership* 9 (Winter 1988): 13.

[23]Thoburn and Balswick, "Prevention Approach," p. 46.

[24]Ibid.

[25]Robert Hemfelt, Frank Minirth and Paul Meier, *Love Is a Choice* (Nashville: Thomas Nelson, 1989), p. 165.

[26]Ibid.

[27]Ibid.

[28]Ibid.

[29]Edwin H. Friedman, *Generation to Generation: Family Process in Church and Synagogue* (New York: Guilford, 1985), pp. 217-18.

[30]Ibid., p. 218.

[31]Rutter, *Sex in the Forbidden Zone*, pp. 7, 55.

[32]See Donna Sinclair, "New Policy Cracks Down on Sexual Abuse," *United Church Observer* 56 (November 1992): 13-14.

[33]See Gerald May, *Care of Mind, Care of Spirit* (San Francisco: Harper & Row, 1982), p. 112.

[34]Don S. Browning, *The Moral Context of Pastoral Care* (Philadelphia: Westminster, 1976), p. 20.

[35]Diane Marshall, "Sexuality and Professional Abuse of Power," *IFL Reflections*, Spring 1991, p. 1.

[36]Joy Jordan-Lake, "Conduct Unbecoming a Preacher," *Christianity Today* 36 (February 10, 1992): 28.

[37]Rutter, *Sex in the Forbidden Zone,* pp. 116-17.

[38]Jack Balswick and John Thoburn, "How Ministers Deal with Sexual Temptation," *Pastoral Psychology* 39 (1991): 278.

[39]Stan Skarsten, "Reflections of a Male Therapist," *IFL Reflections,* Spring 1991, p. 3.

[40]Ibid.

[41]Steinke, "Clergy Affairs," p. 56.

[42]Patrick Carnes, *Out of the Shadows* (Minneapolis: CompCare, 1983), p. 4.

[43]Ibid., p. 9.

[44]Ibid., p. 4.

[45]Ibid., p. 6.

[46]Ibid., p. 24.

[47]John White, *Eros Defiled: The Christian and Sexual Sin* (Downers Grove, Ill.: InterVarsity Press, 1977), p. 94.

[48]William H. Masters, Virginia E. Johnson and Robert C. Kolodny, *Sex and Human Loving* (Boston: Little, Brown, 1982), p. 376.

[49]Ibid., p. 263.

[50]Tim Stafford, "Great Sex: Reclaiming a Christian Sexual Ethic," *Christianity Today* 31 (October 2, 1987): 43.

[51]Masters, Johnson and Kolodny, *Sex and Human Loving,* p. 376.

[52]Ibid., p. 30.

[53]Patrick Carnes, *Don't Call It Love: Recovery from Sexual Addiction* (London: Judy Piatkus, 1991), p. 22.

[54]According to the survey, 38 percent of pastors fantasize once a month or more often, whereas 26 percent of laypersons engage in this activity. Stafford, "Great Sex," p. 26.

Chapter 3: Misconduct as Betrayal of a Sexual Trust

[1]A difference in the relative power of each person in a relationship marks the difference between sexual advance and sexual harassment. Hence "harassment is a sexual advance by one who is in a position of power and where there is either explicit or implicit in the advance a threat to use that power in some form." Karen Lebacqz and Ronald G. Barton, *Sex in the Parish* (Louisville, Ky.: Westminster/John Knox, 1991), p. 137.

[2]John Theis, "Power and Sexual Abuse in the Roman Catholic Church," *Grail* 8 (December 1992): 48.

[3]Pamela Cooper-White, "Soul Stealing: Power and Relations in Pastoral Sexual Abuse," *The Christian Century* 108 (February 20, 1991): 199.

[4]However, as Marie Fortune notes, sexual activity and sexual violence are ethical opposites, for true sexual activity requires the "informed and freely chosen agreement" of both persons and not merely submission to a greater power or authority. Marie Marshall Fortune, *Sexual Violence: The Unmentionable Sin* (New York: Pilgrim, 1983), p. 35.

[5]Stan Skarsten, "Reflections of a Male Therapist," *IFL Reflections*, Spring 1991, p. 3.

[6]Theis, "Power and Sexual Abuse," p. 48.

[7]Ibid., p. 49.

[8]For a fuller development of the biblical understanding of sexuality, see Stanley J. Grenz, *Sexual Ethics* (Dallas: Word, 1990), pp. 3-80, 159-76.

[9]For a characterization of this view by an opponent, see Philip Turner, *Sex, Money and Power* (Cambridge, Mass.: Cowley, 1985), pp. 35-37.

[10]Richard Hettlinger, *Sex Isn't That Simple: The New Sexuality on Campus* (New York: Seabury, 1974), p. 80.

[11]Maslow notes the implications of this understanding: "It would appear that no single sexual act can per se be called abnormal or perverted. It is only abnormal or perverted individuals who can commit abnormal or perverted acts. That is, the dynamic meaning of the act is far more important than the act itself." Abraham Maslow, "Self-Esteem (Dominance-Feeling) and Sexuality in Women," in *Sexual Behavior and Personality Characteristics*, ed. M. F. DeMartino (New York: Grove, 1966), p. 103.

[12]For an important example of those who reject the viability of the older ethic, see Lebacqz and Burton, *Sex in the Parish*, p. 241.

[13]Fortune, *Sexual Violence*, p. 100.

[14]Ibid., p. 101.

[15]Don S. Browning, *The Moral Context of Pastoral Care* (Philadelphia: Westminster, 1976), pp. 97-98.

[16]Ibid.

[17]Lewis Smedes, *Caring and Commitment* (San Francisco: Harper & Row, 1988), pp. 128, 130.

[18]Tim O'Connell, "The Look of a Happy Priest," as quoted in David Rice, *Shattered Vows: Exodus from the Priesthood* (Belfast: Blackstaff, 1990), pp. 146-47.

[19]A. W. Richard Sipe, *A Secret World: Sexuality and the Search for Celibacy* (New York: Brunner/Mazel, 1990), pp. 266-77.

[20]Fortune, *Sexual Violence*, p. 84.

[21]Charles L. Rassieur, *The Problem Clergymen Don't Talk About* (Philadelphia: Westminster Press, 1976), p. 63.

Chapter 4: Misconduct as Betrayal of a Power Trust

[1]John D. Vogelsang, "From Denial to Hope: A Systemic Response to Clergy Sexual Abuse," *Journal of Religion and Health* 32 (Fall 1993): 197.

[2]Pamela Cooper-White, "Soul Stealing: Power and Relations in Pastoral Sexual Abuse," *The Christian Century* 108 (February 20, 1991): 199.

[3]Bill Schmidt, "Underlying Attitudes," *PMC* 9 (May 1992): 4.

[4]Gary A. Yukl, *Leadership in Organizations*, 2nd ed. (Englewood Cliffs, N.J.: Prentice-Hall, 1989), p. 12.

[5]Sidney I. Landau, ed., *The Doubleday Dictionary for Home, School and Office* (Garden City,

N.Y.: Doubleday, 1975), p. 48.

[6]*Funk and Wagnalls New Standard Dictionary of the English Language* (New York: Funk and Wagnalls, 1965), 1:193.

[7]Ibid., 2:1946.

[8]Landau, *Doubleday Dictionary*, p. 569.

[9]Yukl, *Leadership in Organizations*, p. 14.

[10]Max Weber, *Economy and Society*, ed. Guenther Roth and Claus Wittich (Los Angeles: University of California Press, 1978), 2:942.

[11]Hence John F. O'Grady, "Authority and Power: Issues for the Contemporary Church," *Louvain Studies* 10 (1984): 123. See also Madeleine Boucher, "Ecumenical Documents: Authority in Community," *Midstream* 21 (July 1982): 405.

[12]For a discussion of the sources of power, see Yukl, *Leadership in Organizations*, pp. 14-15. For an alternative summary see John Kenneth Galbraith, *The Anatomy of Power* (Boston: Houghton Mifflin, 1983), pp. 6-7.

[13]See David K. Switzer, *Pastor, Preacher, Person: Developing a Pastoral Ministry in Depth* (Nashville: Abingdon, 1979), pp. 17-19.

[14]Paul Tillich, *Dynamics of Faith* (New York: Harper & Brothers, 1957), pp. 41-43.

[15]Switzer, *Pastor, Preacher, Person*, p. 18.

[16]Ibid.

[17]Karen Lebacqz, *Professional Ethics: Power and Paradox* (Nashville: Abingdon, 1985), p. 121.

[18]See ibid., p. 111.

[19]For an extended discussion of this problem, see James Newton Poling, *The Abuse of Power: A Theological Problem* (Nashville: Abingdon, 1991).

[20]For a helpful discussion of this, see Karen Lebacqz and Ronald G. Barton, *Sex in the Parish* (Louisville, Ky.: Westminster/John Knox, 1991), pp. 121-24.

[21]Peter Rutter, *Sex in the Forbidden Zone: When Men in Power—Therapists, Doctors, Clergy, Teachers and Others—Betray Women's Trust* (Los Angeles: Jeremy P. Tarcher, 1989), p. 25.

[22]Ibid., p. 124.

[23]Lebacqz and Barton, *Sex in the Parish*, p. 124.

[24]Marie M. Fortune, *Is Nothing Sacred? When Sex Invades the Pastoral Relationship* (San Francisco: Harper & Row, 1992) p. 42.

[25]Rutter, *Sex in the Forbidden Zone*, p. 21.

[26]Ruth Tiffany Barnhouse, *Clergy and the Sexual Revolution* (Washington, D.C.: Alban Institute, 1987), p. 32.

[27]See Lebacqz and Barton, *Sex in the Parish*, pp. 122-23; Rutter, *Sex in the Forbidden Zone*, p. 51.

[28]Marie Marshall Fortune, *Sexual Violence: The Unmentionable Sin* (New York: Pilgrim, 1983), p. 110.

[29]Vogelsang, "From Denial to Hope," p. 199. This is confirmed in the stories of the

women abused by "Peter Donovan" cited in Fortune, *Is Nothing Sacred?* pp. 12-45.

[30]Fortune, *Sexual Violence,* pp. 107-108.

[31]Fortune, *Is Nothing Sacred?* p. 37.

[32]Galbraith, *Anatomy of Power,* pp. 4-6, 14-37.

[33]Ibid., p. 3.

[34]Ibid., pp. 5-6.

[35]Don Basham, *Lead Us Not into Temptation* (Old Tappan, N.J.: Chosen Books, 1986), p. 63.

[36]Fortune, *Is Nothing Sacred?* p. 121.

[37]Switzer, *Pastor, Preacher, Person,* pp. 34-35.

[38]Schmidt, "Underlying Attitudes," p. 5.

[39]Ibid.

[40]Switzer, *Pastor, Preacher, Person,* pp. 16-17.

[41]Schmidt, "Underlying Attitudes," p. 5.

[42]Lebacqz and Barton, *Sex in the Parish,* p. 124.

[43]Dean C. Ludwig and Clinton O. Longenecker, "The Bathsheba Syndrome: The Ethical Failure of Successful Leaders," *Journal of Business Ethics* 12 (April 1993): 268.

[44]Ibid., p. 268.

[45]Ibid., p. 269.

[46]Ibid., p. 271.

[7]For a discussion of this phenomenon, see Janet Fishburn, "Male Clergy Adultery as Vocational Confusion," *The Christian Century* 99 (September 15-22, 1982): 922-25.

[48]Barnhouse, *Clergy and the Sexual Revolution,* p. 33.

[49]Gerhard von Rad, "Eikon," in the *Theological Dictionary of the New Testament,* ed. Gerhard Kittel, trans. Geoffrey W. Bromiley (Grand Rapids, Mich.: Eerdmans, 1964), 2:392. See also Henri Blocher, *In the Beginning: The Opening Chapters of Genesis,* trans. David G. Preston (Leicester, U.K.: Inter-Varsity Press, 1984), p. 81.

[50]For a development of the philosophical basis for the social understanding of personhood, see Alistair I. McFadyen, *The Call to Personhood: A Christian Theory of the Individual in Social Relationships* (Cambridge: Cambridge University Press, 1990).

[51]See Glenn Tinder, *The Political Meaning of Christianity* (San Francisco: HarperCollins, 1991), pp. 20-21.

Chapter 5: Ministering to the Victims of Misconduct

[1]This case is described by Andre Bustanoby, "Counseling the Seductive Female," *Leadership* 9 (Winter 1988): 48.

[2]Ibid., pp. 49-50.

[3]Ibid., p. 49.

[4]Marie M. Fortune, *Is Nothing Sacred? When Sex Invades the Pastoral Relationship* (San Francisco: Harper & Row, 1992) p. xv.

[5]Ibid.

[6]Ibid., p. xviii.

[7]J. Steven Muse, "Faith, Hope and the 'Urge to Merge' in Pastoral Ministry: Some Countertransference-Related Distortions of Relationship Between Male Pastors and Their Female Parishioners," *Journal of Pastoral Care* 46 (Fall 1992): 303-6.

[8]Ibid., p. 303.

[9]Ibid.

[10]Ibid., p. 305.

[11]Ibid., p. 306.

[12]Fortune, *Is Nothing Sacred?* p. 115.

[13]Ibid., p. 66.

[14]Willard Gaylin, *The Killing of Bonnie Garland* (New York: Simon & Schuster, 1982), p. 330.

[15]Ibid.

[16]David Stoop and James Masteller, *Forgiving Our Parents, Forgiving Ourselves* (Ann Arbor, Mich.: Servant, 1991), p. 205.

[17]Ibid., p. 179.

[18]Roy M. Oswald, "Clergy Stress," *The Alban Institute Action Information*, March/April 1984, p. 11.

[19]Ibid.

[20]Ibid.

[21]Philip Blumstein and Pepper Schwartz, *American Couples* (New York: Morrow, 1984), p. 174.

[22]Ibid., p. 175.

[23]David and Vera Mace, *What's Happening to Clergy Marriages?* (Nashville: Abingdon, 1980), p. 40.

[24]Ibid., p. 30.

[25]Ibid., p. 41.

[26]Heather Bryce, "After the Affair: A Wife's Story," *Leadership* 9 (Winter 1988): 64.

[27]Ibid.

[28]Douglas Todd, "The Beginning of the End: Former Evangelical Minister Who Preached Against Homosexuality Now Dying of AIDS," *Vancouver Sun*, January 13, 1994, p. A1.

[29]Ibid.

[30]"Ghost in the Bedroom," *Canadian Baptist* 141 (January 1995): 17-18.

[31]Ibid.

[32]Ibid.

Chapter 6: The Pastor & the Prevention of Misconduct

[1]Jack Balswick and John Thoburn, "How Ministers Deal with Sexual Temptation," *Pastoral Psychology* 39 (1991): 285.

[2]John Theis, "Power and Sexual Abuse in the Roman Catholic Church," *Grail* 8 (De-

cember 1992): 39.

[3]Teresa L. Tribe and Douglas R. Wilson, "Taken for Granted," *PMC* 9 (May 1992): 19.

[4]Peter Rutter, *Sex in the Forbidden Zone: When Men in Power—Therapists, Doctors, Clergy, Teachers and Others—Betray Women's Trust* (Los Angeles: Jeremy P. Tarcher, 1989), pp. 57-61.

[5]Robert J. Carlson, "Battling Sexual Indiscretion," *Ministry* 60 (January 1987): 5.

[6]Balswick and Thoburn, "How Ministers Deal with Sexual Temptation," p. 280.

[7]Ibid., p. 270.

[8]Stan Skarsten, "Reflections of a Male Therapist," *IFL Reflections*, Spring 1991, p. 3.

[9]Tribe and Wilson, "Taken for Granted," p. 20.

[10]Don Basham, *Lead Us Not into Temptation* (Old Tappan, N.J.: Chosen Books, 1986), p. 100.

[11]J. Steven Muse, "Faith, Hope and the 'Urge to Merge' in Pastoral Ministry: Some Countertransference-Related Distortions of Relationship Between Male Pastors and Their Female Parishioners," *Journal of Pastoral Care* 46 (Fall 1992): 299-300.

[12]Ibid., p. 299.

[13]For a helpful description of the purposes of pastoral care, see J. Russell Burck, "Pastoral Care and Clergy Ethics," in *Clergy Ethics in a Changing Society: Mapping the Terrain*, ed. James P. Wind et al. (Louisville, Ky.: Westminster/John Knox, 1991), pp. 178-97.

[14]Muse, "Faith, Hope and the 'Urge to Merge,' " p. 299.

[15]Walter E. Wiest and Elwyn A. Smith, *Ethics in Ministry: A Guide for the Professional* (Minneapolis: Fortress, 1990), p. 186.

[16]For an example see Janice Russell, *Out of Bounds* (London: Sage, 1993), pp. 112-22.

[17]John D. Vogelsang, "Reconstructing the Professional at the End of Modernity," *Journal of Religion and Health* 33 (Spring 1994): 68.

[18]J. Andrew Cole, "Eroticized Psychotherapy and Its Management: A Clinical Illustration," *Journal of Psychology and Christianity* 12 (1993): 263.

[19]Pamela Cooper-White, "Soul Stealing: Power and Relations in Pastoral Sexual Abuse," *The Christian Century* 108 (February 20, 1991): 197.

[20]James DeBoe, "Personality-Splitting Trauma," *Perspectives* 7 (September 1992): 14.

[21]Kathi Carino, "A Dark Room in My Mind," *Perspectives* 7 (September 1992): 10.

[22]Ibid., pp. 11-12.

[23]Maxine Glaz, "Reconstructing the Pastoral Care of Women," *Second Opinion* 17 (1991): 98.

[24]Jeff T. Seat, James T. Trent and Iwa K. Kim, "The Prevalence and Contributing Factors of Sexual Misconduct Among Southern Baptist Pastors in Six Southern States," *Journal of Pastoral Care* 47 (Winter 1993): 369.

[25]For example, Muse, "Faith, Hope and the 'Urge to Merge,' " pp. 306-7; Karen Lebacqz and Ronald G. Barton, *Sex in the Parish* (Louisville, Ky.: Westminster/John Knox, 1991), p. 65.

[26]These are based on California legal guidelines for psychologists. See Carl Sherman,

"Behind Closed Doors: Therapist-Client Sex," *Psychology Today* 26 (May/June 1993): 64-72.

[27]Rutter, *Sex in the Forbidden Zone*, p. 223.

[28]Cole, "Eroticized Psychotherapy and Its Management," p. 263.

[29]Rutter, *Sex in the Forbidden Zone*, p. 223.

[30]Cole, "Eroticized Psychotherapy and Its Management," p. 263.

Chapter 7: The Church's Response to Misconduct

[1]Marie M. Fortune, *Is Nothing Sacred? When Sex Invades the Pastoral Relationship* (San Francisco: Harper & Row, 1992), p. xiv.

[2]This case forms the foundation for the discussion in ibid.

[3]Ibid., p. 49.

[4]Ibid., p. 50.

[5]Donald Capps, "Sex in the Parish: Social Scientific Explanation for Why It Occurs," *Journal of Pastoral Care* 47 (Winter 1993): 354.

[6]Ibid., p. 354.

[7]Ibid., p. 355.

[8]Ibid., p. 357.

[9]Ibid., p. 356.

[10]Ibid., p. 360.

[11]Ibid., p. 359.

[12]Gordon Fee, *1 and 2 Timothy, Titus*, New International Commentary (Peabody, Mass.: Hendrickson, 1984), p. 130.

[13]In the United States, the United Methodist Church, the Christian Reformed Church, the Presbyterian Church U.S.A., the U.S. Conference of the Mennonite Brethren, the Evangelical Lutheran Church in America, and the Episcopal Church have attempted to devise a means of dealing with offenses. "Misconduct Policies Issued," *Christianity Today* 37 (January 11, 1993): 48.

[14]See Debra Fieguth, "After All These Years," *Faith Today*, March/April 1994, p. 29.

[15]Nancy R. Heisey, "Another Look at Matthew 18," *The Mennonite* 107 (October 27, 1992): 466-67.

[16]Ibid., p. 467.

[17]See Fieguth, "After All These Years," pp. 29-30.

[18]Ibid., p. 11.

[19]Ibid., p. 47.

[20]Fortune, *Is Nothing Sacred?* p. 115.

[21]Ibid., p. 126.

[22]Roger Bryant, "I Committed Adultery," *Ministry* 65 (July 1992): 13.

[23]Judith Karman, "Healing the Wounded Pastor in a Dysfunctional World," *Fuller Focus* 11 (Winter 1993): 23.

[24]Source withheld by request.

[25]David Turner and Max R. Uhlemann, eds., *A Legal Handbook for the Helping Professional* (Vancouver: Law Foundation of British Columbia, 1991), p. 44.

[26]*Church Law and Tax Report*, May/June 1989 (Matthews, N.C.: Christian Ministry Resources), as quoted in an unpublished draft, "Pastoral Misconduct Workshop," American Baptist Churches U.S.A., January 1993.

[27]Peter Rutter, *Sex in the Forbidden Zone: When Men in Power—Therapists, Doctors, Clergy, Teachers and Others—Betray Women's Trust* (Los Angeles: Jeremy P. Tarcher, 1989), p. 223.

Chapter 8: Hope for the Wanderer

[1]J. E. B., "The Commentary," *Evangelicals Now* (November 1999).

[2]Virginia Satir, *People Making* (Palo Alto, Calif.: Science and Behavior Books, 1972).

[3]Ibid., p. 17.

[4]Michael McManus, *Marriage Savers* (Grand Rapids, Mich.: Zondervan, 1993), p. 171.

[5]Ibid.

[6]Ibid., p. 172.

[7]Ibid.

[8]John Gottman, *Why Marriages Succeed or Fail* (New York: Simon & Schuster, 1994).

[9]John Gottman, *The Seven Principles for Making Marriage Work* (New York: Crown Publishers, 1999).

[10]Gottman, *Why Marriages Succeed or Fail*, p. 28.

[11]Ibid., p. 29.

[12]Gottman, *Seven Principles*, p. 27.

[13]Ibid.

[14]Cameron Lee and Jack Balswick, *Life in a Glass House* (Grand Rapids, Mich.: Zondervan, 1989), p. 161.

[15]Ibid., p. 209.

[16]Ibid., p. 217.

[17]Frank Pittman, *Private Lies: Infidelity and the Betrayal of Intimacy* (New York: Norton, 1989).

[18]Clifford L. Penner and Joyce J. Penner, *Restoring the Pleasure* (Dallas: Word, 1993), p. 32.

[19]Donald R. Harvey, *The Spiritually Intimate Marriage* (Tarrytown, N.Y.: Fleming H. Revell, 1991).

[20]Ibid., p. 19.

[21]Ibid., p. 20.

[22]Ibid., p. 45.

[23]Ibid.

[24]Ibid., p. 162.

[25]Pittman, *Private Lies*, p. 32.

[26]Gerald Carey, *Theory and Practice of Counseling and Psychotherapy* (Pacific Grove: Brooks/Cole Publishing, 1991).

[27]Ibid., p. 331.

[28]Henry Cloud and John Townsend, *Boundaries* (Grand Rapids, Mich.: Zondervan, 1992), p. 42.

[29]Ibid., p. 103.

[30]Barbara Killinger, *Workaholics: The Respectable Addiction* (Toronto, Ontario: Kay Porter Books, 1992).

[31]Ibid., p. 7.

The authors of this book combine a rich world of pastoral work and graduate teaching experience. **Stanley J. Grenz,** Pioneer McDonald Professor of Theology and Ethics at Carey Theological College and Regent College (Vancouver), is one of the foremost evangelical theologians in North America today. He is the author of over twenty books, including *Created for Community: Connecting Christian Belief with Christian Living* and *Renewing the Center: Evangelical Theology in a Post-Theological Era.* **Roy D. Bell** is retired but most recently served as Erb/Gullison Professor of Family Ministries, also at Carey Theological College.